T0295939

Talent Strategies and Leadership Development of the Public Sector

To stay ahead of the competition, the public sector has to ensure an effective talent management strategy to attract, develop and retain talents. Effective talent management is about aligning the organisation's approach to talent with the strategic aims and purpose of the organisation. This book adopts a comparative country analysis, which takes into account the institutional emphasis, organisational configuration and unique characteristics of the public sector.

Against the backdrop of three major stages of administrative development, i.e., the colonial, postcolonial and modern periods, this book unpacks how the talent schemes have been shaped by the reforms, experiences, cross-country knowledge transfers and evolved over time responding to globalisation and digitalisation in Southeast Asia.

This book will be of great interest to scholars and public managers working on public administration and civil service reforms in Asia towards developing a contextualised understanding of talent management and leadership development in the region.

Celia Lee is Research Fellow at Nanyang Technological University, Singapore. Formerly a practitioner in the Singapore public sector, her research interests include Talent Strategies in the Public Sector (Asia); Transnational Knowledge Transfer; Public Sector Innovation; Governance in the Philanthropy Sector; BRI and ASEAN.

Routledge Focus on Public Governance in Asia

Series Editors:

Hong Liu
Nanyang Technological University, Singapore

Wenxuan Yu
Xiamen University, China

Focusing on new governance challenges, practices and experiences in and about a globalizing Asia, particularly East Asia and Southeast Asia, this focus series invites upcoming and established researchers all over the world to succinctly and comprehensively discuss important public administration and policy themes such as government administrative reform, public budgeting reform, government crisis management, public–private partnership, science and technology policy, technology-enabled public service delivery, public health and aging, talent management and anti-corruption across Asian countries. The book series presents compact and concise content under 50,000 words long which has significant theoretical contributions to the governance theory with an Asian perspective and practical implications for administration and policy reform and innovation.

Exploring Public-Private Partnerships in Singapore
The Success-Failure Continuum
Soojin Kim and Kai Xiang Kwa

Collaborative Governance of Local Governments in China
Jing Cui

Local Government Innovativeness in China
Youlang Zhang

**Talent Strategies and Leadership Development
of the Public Sector**
Insights from Southeast Asia
Celia Lee

For more information about this series, please visit www.routledge.com/ Routledge-Focus-on-Public-Governance-in-Asia/book-series/RFPGA

Talent Strategies and Leadership Development of the Public Sector
Insights from Southeast Asia

Celia Lee

Routledge
Taylor & Francis Group

LONDON AND NEW YORK

First published 2021
by Routledge
2 Park Square, Milton Park, Abingdon, Oxon OX14 4RN

and by Routledge
605 Third Avenue, New York, NY 10158

Routledge is an imprint of the Taylor & Francis Group, an informa business

© 2021 Celia Lee

British Library Cataloguing-in-Publication Data
A catalogue record for this book is available from the British
Library

Library of Congress Cataloging-in-Publication Data
Names: Lee, Celia, author.
Title: Talent strategies and leadership development of the
    public sector : insights from Southeast Asia / Celia Lee.
Description: Abingdon, Oxon ; New York, NY : Routledge, 2022. |
    Series: Routledge focus on public governance in Asia | Includes
    bibliographical references and index.
Identifiers: LCCN 2021007893 | ISBN 9780367862244 (hardback) |
    ISBN 9781003017776 (ebook)
Subjects: LCSH: Civil service—Southeast Asia—Personnel
    management. | Civil service reform—Southeast Asia. |
    Public officers—Training of—Southeast Asia. | Leadership—
    Southeast Asia.
Classification: LCC JQ750.A69 P445 2022 | DDC 352.6/
    690959—dc23
LC record available at https://lccn.loc.gov/2021007893

ISBN: 978-0-367-86224-4 (hbk)
ISBN: 978-1-032-05320-2 (pbk)
ISBN: 978-1-003-01777-6 (ebk)

Typeset in Galliard
by Apex CoVantage, LLC

Contents

Tables and figures

Tables

Figures

Acknowledgements

The research of this book was supported by the Singapore Ministry of Education AcRF Tier-2 Grant entitled 'Transnational Knowledge Transfer and Dynamic Governance in Comparative Perspective' [MOE2016-T2–02–87].

Many thanks to the public officials from the various agencies in Singapore, Malaysia, Thailand, Cambodia and Vietnam who have participated in this research either through face-to-face interviews or administered through questionnaires.

Preface

Since the term 'war for talent' was first coined in 1998 by McKinsey (Michaels et al., 2001), the idea of talent management was quickly adopted by many human resource management specialists as the solution to overcome the increasingly fierce competition to attract, retain and harness talents. Furthermore, talent management research has drawn the interest of many researchers as a way to build human capacity. Yet, academic research in the field of TM does not give much support in finding the right talent management solutions and has mainly focused on large organisations in the private sector for the past decades (Thunnissen et al., 2013; Powell et al., 2012; Gallardo-Gallardo & Thunnissen, 2015; Buttiens & Hondeghem, 2015). Despite the increasing scholarly attention for Talent Management during the past 10 years (Thunnissen et al., 2013), and especially over the course of the past few years (Gallardo-Gallardo & Thunnissen, 2015), there is still no consensus over its definition, theoretical background and scope.

Against the backdrop of the three major stages of administrative development, i.e., the colonial, postcolonial and current modern periods, this book will unpack and explore how the talent schemes in the respective countries have been shaped by the reforms, experiences and cross-country knowledge transfers within the Southeast Asia region, of which many of the concepts and theories are borrowed from the western nations influenced by the New Public Management (Hood, 1991) movement. Talent management practices are largely informed by the hegemony of human resource management models developed in the private sector. Beyond cross-national variations in the degree of adopting imitative models, this reality of borrowed administrative models has major implications for the leadership development of senior public administrators in Southeast Asia.

This book will be of great interest to scholars and public managers working on public administration and civil service reforms in Asia towards developing a contextualised understanding of talent management and leadership development in the region which corresponds to the stage of development.

Celia Lee is Research Fellow at the Nanyang Centre for Public Administration, Nanyang Technological University, Singapore. Formerly a practitioner in the Singapore public sector, her research interests include Talent Strategies in the Public Sector (Asia); Transnational Knowledge Transfer; Public SEctor Innovation; Governance in the Philanthropy Sector; BRI and ASEAN.

Introduction

Since the term 'war for talent' was first coined in 1998 by McKinsey (Michaels et al., 2001), the idea of talent management was quickly adopted by many human resource management specialists as the solution to overcome the increasingly fierce competition to attract, retain and harness talents. Furthermore, talent management research has drawn the interest of many researchers as a way to build human capacity. Yet, academic research in the field of TM does not give much support in finding the right talent management solutions and has mainly focused on large organisations in the private sector for the past decades (Thunnissen et al., 2013; Powell et al., 2012; Gallardo-Gallardo & Thunnissen, 2015; Buttiens & Hondeghem, 2015). Despite the increasing scholarly attention for talent Management during the past 10 years (Thunnissen et al., 2013), and especially over the course of the past few years (Gallardo-Gallardo & Thunnissen, 2015), there is still no consensus over its definition, theoretical background and scope.

Despite the increasing call to pay attention to talent management in the public sector, it is still an underexplored research area. Most of the research in the public sector also stems from consultancy reports which provide recommendations, based on the private sector experience, of how and why the public sector could benefit from TM (e.g., Hays, 2012). Some have attempted to investigate talent management's possible conceptualisation (e.g., Harris and Foster, 2010), operationalisation (e.g., Thunnissen and Buttiens, 2017), success (e.g., Clarke & Scurry, 2017), dimensions in the institutional environment and influence of stakeholders (Buttiens & Hondeghem, 2015), and its mechanisms of overcoming its challenging application to the public sector (Reilly, 2008). Although there has been a growth of empirical studies in the public sector, most of them are also based on a Western context. Hence, talent management in the public sector remains largely underexplored in an Asian context. As we witnessed the rise of Asia in contrast to the declining confidence in the Western powers, it is time to explore the contextualised lessons of Asian countries' TM practices to uncover emerging talent management models in Asia.

Southeast Asia, in particular, has witnessed major theoretical, structural, functional and ethical reforms in the public administration in the recent two decades (Haque, 2004). In the region, from the colonial bureaucratic administrative system to the state-driven mode of public administration that emerged post-independence, it has evolved into an enterprise like public management and towards consultative policy advocacy. Public sector reforms are changes in government processes or structures that help to achieve economic developments and address key public policy challenges. Some processes are directly linked to citizens with regard to the mode of service delivery, while others are less visible to citizens but are no less salient to those working 'on the inside' of government. As the public sector is responsible for designing and monitoring policy practices, decisions made by the public sector will have an impact on the people and credibility of the government (Taylor & Wright, 2004). Therefore, it is important to attract, develop and retain key potential talented public servants to successfully bring the country through the reforms and smooth transformations of the economies. Confronted with a chronic shortage of talented people within the current global landscape of skills shortages, changing demographics, increasing austerity and uncertainties, public sectors around the world are facing intensified competition for talents. To stay ahead of the competition, the public sector has to ensure an effective talent management strategy and consider leadership developments for the competent employees with the most potential for succession planning. Successful talent management and leadership development are achieved by balancing knowledge exchange, action, reflection and alignment.

Against the backdrop of three major stages of administrative development, i.e., the colonial, postcolonial and current modern periods, The *Talent Strategies and Leadership Development of the Public Sector: Insights from Southeast Asia* will unpack how the talent schemes in the respective countries have been shaped by the reforms, experiences and cross-country knowledge transfers within the Southeast Asia region, of which many of the concepts and theories are borrowed from the western nations influenced by the New Public Management (Hood, 1991) movement. In particular, talent management practices are largely informed by the hegemony of human resource management models developed in the private sector. Beyond cross-national variations in the degree of adopting imitative models, this reality of borrowed administrative models has major implications for the leadership development of senior public administrators in Southeast Asia, especially in terms of their external intellectual and professional dependence as well as the challenge to reconcile foreign models with unique local conditions. In addition, the borrowed western models as well as the externally imposed socialist structures have created elitist talent schemes that evoked tensions between inclusiveness and exclusiveness of talent management practices based on social isolationism.

Unpacking talent management in the public sector

The aim of talent management within the public sector is to provide pools of public servants with outstanding characteristics to serve the public and stakeholders and sustain competitive advantage in the long run (EPU, 2016). Confronted with a chronic shortage of talented people within the current global landscape of skills shortages, changing demographics, increasing austerity and uncertainties, public sectors around the world are facing intensified competition for talents. Governments are constantly striving to recruit, retain, reward, and develop their pool of public employees but they face fierce competition with the higher-paying private sector. However, the public sector is not the most sought-after employer – Google, Apple and Microsoft were the top three employer brands according to the World's Most Attractive Employers research in 2020 (Universum, 2020).

When governments cannot recruit and retain capable individuals, it adds to the vicious cycle of weak governance. With the widespread practice of performance management in the public sector, the 'war for talent' is the top agenda for civil services around the world (Kim, 2008; Van Dijk, 2009). For bureaucracies to be staffed by the best-talented people, governments have intervened by establishing a variety of talent programmes or schemes such as the United States' Senior Executive Service, the United Kingdom's Fast Stream, South Korea's Senior Civil Service, Singapore's Administrative Services, Thailand's High Performance and Potential System, and Malaysia's Administrative and Diplomatic schemes. These programmes targeted at selected individuals being identified at an early stage of their career and are developed further through trainings, job rotations, mentorships, projects etc. to become future leaders (Dries, 2013; Poocharoen & Lee, 2013; McNulty & Kaveri, 2019). However, some of these schemes are more successful in some contexts and have been perceived as inequitable and unfair. Such a system has also been criticised to breed elitism and distort behaviours of civil servants. There is also the gradual moving away from the seniority-based promotion towards performance-based frameworks, but there are complexities of developing standards and measures of performance, distinguishing individual versus group performance and short-term output versus long-term outcome.

Such selectivity and ambiguities that affect talent policies and practices in the public sector have led to tensions in the operationalisation of talent management within the exclusivity versus inclusivity conundrum. Empirical research on talent management in the public sector has pointed out that talent management in public sectors of different countries, whether inclusive or exclusive, very much depends on context. In the case of Southeast Asia, the context is dependent on its development stage.

Why this book?

This book *Talent Strategies and Leadership Development of the Public Sector: A Study of Talent Schemes in Singapore, Malaysia* acknowledges that present-day knowledge about talent management in the public sector especially in Southeast Asia is quite scarce and underexplored. The studies also seldom focus on how the administrative reform has shaped talent schemes and leadership development. Given the current state of global knowledge on the public sector as we witnessed the rise of Asia in contrast to the declining confidence in the West, it is timely to explore the contextualised lessons of Asian countries' TM practices. This will uncover emerging talent management and leadership development models in Asia especially in an era of increasing globalisation and digitisation. This book will be of great interest to scholars and public managers working on public administration and civil service reforms in Asia towards developing a contextualised understanding of talent management and leadership development in the region which corresponds to the stage of development.

Southeast Asia is an interesting region to focus on talent management and leadership development because of its common colonial roots which have influenced the region's public administration. The region is situated east of the Indian subcontinent and south of China. Southeast Asia stretches some 4,000 miles at its greatest extent (roughly from northwest to southeast) and encompasses some 5,000,000 square miles (13,000,000 square km) of land and sea, of which about 1,736,000 square miles is land. Mainland Southeast Asia is divided into the countries of Cambodia, Laos, Myanmar (Burma), Thailand, Vietnam, and the small city-state of Singapore at the southern tip of the Malay Peninsula; Cambodia, Laos, and Vietnam, which occupy the eastern portion of the mainland, often are collectively called the Indochinese Peninsula. Malaysia is both mainland and insular, with a western portion on the Malay Peninsula and an eastern part on the island of Borneo. Except for the small sultanate of Brunei (also on Borneo), the remainder of insular Southeast Asia consists of the archipelagic nations of Indonesia and the Philippines. Southeast Asia is perhaps the most diverse region with a variety of economic, social and cultural niches; hundreds of ethnic groups, languages and religions. Although the region shared common colonisation background, yet development of each country's level of economic and social development varies with Singapore being the only country that attained developed status and one of the world's highest GDP per capita. Strong governments are needed in the region to ensure economic development and political stability. If the public sector is not able to attract talents, it will add to the vicious cycle of weak governance and low public service quality (Poocharoen & Lee, 2013). Therefore, appropriate talent management practices and leadership development programmes are critical to be designed and implemented in the public sector to attract and retain talents, especially in the 'war for talent' with the private sector.

Given the ongoing public sector reform efforts in Southeast Asia, this book will define talent management in the public sector and provide a detailed analysis of the talent management schemes, practices and leadership development strategies linking to public sector reforms, globalisation and digitalisation in the Southeast Asia region. Globalisation has facilitated the widespread adoption of the western ideology of New Public Management and Reinventing Government, leading to the rise of privatisation movement in the public sector, ending the tenured system of employment. Public servants no longer enjoyed the security formerly associated with the job, which also led to the diminished incentive to join the public sector and an erosion of public servants' commitment and loyalty. Therefore, the public sector organisations are also confronted with the intensifying competition for attracting and retaining the 'best and brightest'. Especially in the digital era, the public sector often is not able to compete with the generous compensation packages offered by the private sector, particularly when recruiting for highly skilled, in-demand professions. The public sector competes with private businesses, academia and tech start-ups for digitally savvy workers as experienced digital developers, data scientists and software engineers may not view the government as an innovator. Attracting digitally savvy workers to the public sector hence is a continuous challenge and without skilled professionals, stubborn issues such as replacing legacy information technology systems, updating infrastructure and improving citizen services are difficult to solve. Although new skills are needed in the new era, agencies also need to retain the deep sector knowledge of existing employees.

It is now common knowledge that when it comes to the 'war for talent' engineers and data scientists have become the hottest resource globally. Today, every organisation needs engineering talent at the helm of all its cross-functional transformation projects. With the accelerating adoption of digital technology and the rise of Artificial Intelligence, the pressure on the talent market for technical skills has vastly increased. Yet, most employers are 'unprepared' and struggle to fill jobs as positions demanding technical skills surge. This is not just due to a shrinking pipeline – with a decreased desire for students to pursue engineering as a profession – but to a competitive landscape that has dramatically changed over the last few years. As governments push ahead to embark on Smart Nation initiatives, it is therefore imperative for governments to continuously hire, groom and train digitally capable talents who can combine technical skills with the understanding of the agency or citizen challenge. The benefits of hiring and retaining top tech personnel in government are massive as investing in tech to bring citizen services up to the 21st-century standards. In addition, the pandemic crisis has also accelerated the adoption of digitalisation in public sectors. Governments have had to expedite their digitalisation efforts to develop digital platforms and solutions not only to deliver services but also to augment their efforts in the tracing and movement control efforts.

Structure of the book

The countries considered in this book include Singapore, Malaysia, Thailand, Cambodia and Vietnam as these are the countries that the author has access to. The findings are derived from semi-structured interviews with public officials, institutes and actors involved in the talent and leadership development process. It is complemented by surveys carried out with former trainees from Thailand, Cambodia and Vietnam who had attended prior executive development programmes for public officials in Singapore. In addition, official documentations, reports and press releases are also included to supplement the interviews and surveys.

The first chapter provides an overview of the three stages of administrative developments, i.e., colonial, postcolonial and modern periods which corresponds to three major models of public administration namely, bureaucratic model, developmental model and 'new public management' model in Southeast Asia. These evolving models have also led to the civil service reforms in the five countries with different unique emphasis in its administration. This will situate reforms relevant to human capacity building and to the adoption of talent management practices. Chapter 2 reviews the developments of talent management literature as a growing discipline in the broader public sector context to provide a clear definition of talent in the public sector which will enrich knowledge and understanding of talent schemes in Southeast Asia. Considering the unique characteristics of the public sector, this chapter will situate the developments of talent management practices within the perspectives of incompatible values and goals of which several stakeholders will have to be accounted for, which might have given rise to tensions along the inclusivity–exclusivity spectrum. The subsequent five chapters (3 to 7) will describe and discuss the talent/career schemes, leadership development programmes and performance management, tracing changes and evolution responding to state of development, demands of citizens and innovative public management in Singapore, Malaysia, Thailand, Cambodia and Vietnam. Chapter 8 compares the various talent management practices and processes at each stage of talent management namely: attraction, development and retention in the five countries to shed light on the impact of institutional emphasis, organisational configurations, characteristics and development stage of the different countries' public sectors. Chapter 9 examines the importance of how transnational learning may assist in transforming public service with a special focus on leadership development of senior-level public servants, particularly looking into learning from overseas governments and jurisdictions that are more advanced that will build the capability of the public services and how learning has shifted from the West-East paradigm to within Asia. Finally, Chapter 10 concludes the book with an assessment of the talent schemes presented in the five countries along the spectrum of inclusivity–exclusivity talent management strategy. This chapter will reflect on the tensions which may arise in the process of implementing talent management practices within well-embedded organisational approaches to equality and diversity in public sector organisations. Finally, it concludes with the recommendation for the shift towards an inclusive approach to talent management to stay ahead in the 'war for talent' with the private sector and responding to the changing context of the public sector.

1 Administrative reforms and transformation in the public sector that shape talent management and leadership development in Southeast Asia

The three public administration models in Southeast Asia: colonial-bureaucratic; postcolonial-development; new public management

In Southeast Asia, we can distinctively discern three models of public administration which corresponded to the various stages of administrative developments. They are colonial-bureaucratic; postcolonial developmental; and the new public management models. These models originated mostly in western nations and were subsequently borrowed by (or imposed on) various countries in the region. Most of the countries adopted or imitated the experiences and models in varying degrees at the different colonial, postcolonial and modern periods, adjusted within the local contexts of these countries (Haque, 2007). Although there existed certain precolonial administrative traditions, such as autocratic-paternalistic rule and kingship-based authority, these were largely transformed or replaced during the colonial rule and postcolonial administrative modernisation. Even for Thailand, which was not under direct colonial rule, its administrative system was also highly influenced by western ideas during the 19th and 20th centuries when the neighbouring countries were under colonial control by the major European powers.

The colonial legacy: from kingship to modern bureaucracy

There were seven major colonial powers in Southeast Asia: Portugal, Spain, the Netherlands, Great Britain, France, the United States, and Japan. From the 1500s to the mid-1940s, colonialism was imposed over Southeast Asia (Osborne, 2000). One interesting feature regarding colonial administration is that it can be dichotomised into two time periods: the administration before the Japanese Occupation and the administration after the Japanese Occupation which was from 1941 to 1945 (Kratoska & Goto,

2015). Both periods are marked by a clear shift in the colonisers' goals regarding their protectorates and the attitudes of the colonised Southeast Asian nations towards their masters.

For centuries, European travellers had been travelling to Southeast Asian countries for trade and economic purposes. They also brought along religion, customs, traditions into the region. The mass immigration caused by the large demand for labour due to the rapidly developed trade and economy had also led to a demographical change in the region. Not only do they have close economic relations with the countries but they also imposed their political domination over a large Southeast Asian territory. Dominant European colonisers such as Great Britain, France, Spain, Portugal and the Netherlands not only occupied the region but also imposed their own goals, interests and style of administration on their colonies (Margolin, 2016; Public Service Division, 2015). Simultaneously, the western political system and education system were brought into the region as well, impacting Southeast Asian political and public administration. The institutions for a modern state such as a state bureaucracy, courts of law were created. The colonial-bureaucratic model offers the guiding principles for modernising administration of the states, replacing traditional kingship institutions which were adopted from South Asia (rajadharma) and West Asia (sultanate).

The two main types of colonial governments in Southeast Asia then were Liberal colonial governments and Repressive colonial governments. The British and the Americans were the two liberal colonial governments at that time but with different administrative models. The British colonised Malaysia, Singapore and Burma, while the Philippines were under the Americans' rule. Under the British rule, the bureaucratic model administration and parliamentary system based on the concept of neutral politics and hierarchal loyalty was established in Malaysia, Singapore and Burma. However, the British's interests regarding governance and talent management negated the interests and demands of the locals. During the colonisation of the Federated Malay States, the pervasiveness of British paternalism resulted in the employment and advancement of British cadets over the local Malays. This practice was ascribed to the belief that the local Malay community, including the educated elites, were neither sufficiently learned nor capable to manage large responsibilities (Wah, 1980). Administrative training was mostly limited to the sons of sultans and chiefs, with some exceptions made for local Malays who proved themselves to be talented. Locals who were recruited into the Malay Administrative Services and the Malayan Civil Service were mostly kept on the lower ranks with low career prospects. While the Philippines under the American's rule adopted the American political system which included the separation of power, the direct election of the President, and the system of checks and balances. The

British and the Americans brought into their colonies the rule of law, civil liberties, and rights in politics.

On the other hand, the Spanish, Dutch and French had more repressive administrative systems. Under the French rule in Cambodia, Laos and Vietnam, a bureaucratic model, headed by a cadre of French officials under a mid-level official recruited by French and the local could become the lower-level officials only. The French language was also imposed as the main language. During the French colonial rule from 1863 to 1953, the protectorate found that the country was civilised with an established gentry with the King at the apex. As such, they initially did not upend the existing administrative structure but they governed through the king (Pike, 2012). Nonetheless, over the years of its colonisation, the French reformed the Cambodian government to suit its goals. In 1887, Cambodia was assimilated into the Indochina Union (besides Laos and the three constituent regions of Vietnam) and the country was stewarded by a Chief Resident (Résident Supérieur). Assistance and counsel on local matters was provided to the Chief Resident by a council of the protectorate consisting of the heads of various public services, such as the offices for agriculture, education, police and penitentiary services, and delegates from the Chambers of Commerce and Agriculture (Prum, 2005).

The Indonesian people's liberty was also limited under the Dutch's ruling. A bureaucracy and a police and military service was established by the Dutch in Indonesia with the aim to maintain social control and to avoid people going against the colonial government. Hence the locals under the repressive ruling by the Spanish, Dutch and French had limited liberty as they were regarded as more superior. Thailand, which was then called Siam, was the only territory that was not colonised by the Europeans. Although it remained as an independent kingdom, its administrative system started to evolve towards the western bureaucratic style as well under the regime of King Chulalongkorn. The reforms based on the western model of administration were also introduced which included uniform standards of public service, arrangement of career services, the principle of neutral politics, and separation between public office and personal life.

Japan's colonisation of Southeast Asia between 1941 and 1945 had both positive and negative effects on the region. While under the Japanese occupation, Southeast Asia underwent major social and economic structural changes. Japan employed the divide and rule tactic in the region which highly disintegrated the region making it more difficult for the countries in this region to implement democratic political systems. Japan's imperialist policy and military dominance exposed the people to many challenges and did not fully favour the social structure of Southeast Asia. Therefore, its failure to develop an effective social and administrative structure made it impossible for it to establish a major impact on Southeast Asia's political system. Its weak political policies and biased development strategies also contributed to heightened social tension, consequently leading to the emergence of new social structures which influenced change in vital social and economic systems in the region. It also evoked anti-Japanese movements and a rising sense of nationalism. Nevertheless, Japan's colonisation had helped to liberate the Southeast Asian region which was dominated by the European bureaucratic elites and formed a new social class that was more business oriented.

Postcolonial administration: rise of nationalism and road to socioeconomic development

Following the Japanese Occupation, the philosophy behind Great Britain's colonial rule shifted from securing its own interests to promoting self-governance in all its colonies. This was to be accomplished through constructing the appropriate institutions and conditions, such as local public service commissions, to nurture the growth of indigenous civil servants and through presenting scholarships to capable local candidates with the aim of preparing them for postings in the higher ranks of the civil service (National Library Board [NLB], 2013). However these institutions were to only be advisory in nature, in that, they are to counsel the Governor, the head of administration in a colony, on the selection and appointment of candidates for posts in the civil service (Tilman, 1961). In 1947, the Trusted Commission published a list of recommendations regarding the creation of a Public Service Commission (PSC). Some of these include, inter alia, the standardisation of administrative schemes into four divisions according to the various prerequisite educational, professional or technical criteria, and the revision of public officers' salaries in the Malayan Union and Singapore (Quah, 2010b). Establishing a PSC was an arduous process for the Federation of Malaya due to the unstable social and political climates at that time. While the Legislative Council looked into the implementation of such an administrative body, an interim organisation known as the Public Service Appointments and Promotions Board was set up with the same basic functions as the PSC in order to test its operability. The interim organisation was further limited to advising the High Commissioner on the selection of candidates for their first appointment to job placements in three of the four divisions that was proposed by the Trusted Commission, and the transfer of current public officers in the same posts. Decision-making regarding six other classes of officers was excluded from the jurisdiction of the interim board. When the Public Services Commission Bill was introduced in 1955 to set up a PSC, it was opposed by the Legislative Council on the grounds

that the Bill did not guarantee the total malayanisation of senior civil service posts within the shortest time possible (Tilman, 1961).

In the hope of maintaining Singapore (part of Malaysia) as a focal point
for Far Eastern imperial defence in the post-war era, some of the local officers were promoted to the senior ranks which were previously monopolised
by European cadets (Low, 2018). On 1 January 1951, Singapore inaugurated its own PSC to safeguard independent control of the nation's bureaucracy from the Malayan Establishment Office, with key operations including
the advising of the local Governor on matters relating to the employment
and promotion of qualified individuals and exercising discipline against err-
ing civil servants (NLB, 2013). A notable restructuring of the Singapore
bureaucratic system began when the British had to content with mount-
ing levels of frustration and national consciousness among the locals for
self-autonomy. Initiating the first step in constitutional reforms was the
commission of the 1953 Rendel Constitution where a system of ministerial
administration was devised to replace some aspects of British colonial governance (Low, 2018). The antagonism of the Legislative Council towards
the creation of a PSC resulted in the interim body's continued operation
till 1957 when the Malay Peninsular obtained the freedom to self-govern
(Public Services Commission of Malaysia, 2020; Tilman, 1961).

After the Japanese Occupation, Cambodia gained a transitory period of
independence under King Norodom Sihanouk in early 1945 with the help
of the Japanese before ultimately ceding to French colonial forces again in
the later part of that year. This attainment of autonomy was symbolic in
nature as the government was dependent on Japanese support and it did
little to improve local conditions. This period was also marked by a coup
between the pro-French royals and loyalists and the pro-Japanese support-
ers. Due to deteriorating political conditions and a desire by the Allies to
defend the nation, the French returned, arrested the Cambodian Prime
Minister, Son Ngoc Thanh, and re-established their regressive colonial
regime (Chandler, 1986; Encyclopaedia Britannica, 2019).

Colonial experience had given rise to anti-colonial as well as anti-fascist
(anti-Japanese aggression) nationalist sentiments that further spawned
independence movements. Southeast Asian elites responded to western
colonialism in a continuum anywhere from adaptation, collaboration, to
resistance. Colonial power's rule upon Southeast Asia had an impact on
the rise of nationalist movements as people tried to fight for their independence. Nationalist movements were triggered to unite local people
against the western powers. Many of these movements were inspired by
western ideologies such as freedom, equality and dignity, influenced by
western education. The rise of modern nationalism in the region can be
credited to capitalist development, the availability of Western education,

the adoption of vernacular languages and the spread of the vernacular press (Gellner, 1983; Anderson, 1991). Emerging native elites were educated in colonial schools and strongly influenced by Western ideals of liberty, socialism and democracy. In Burma, Students from the University of Rangoon formed the Dobayma Asiyone ('We Burman') society in 1935. In Indonesia, Dutch-educated Indonesians formed the Indonesian Nationalist Party (PNI) in 1927 to create a modern state free from Dutch colonial rule. In Singapore, the People's Action Party was formed in 1954 by middle-class English-educated Chinese. Subsequently, PAP led Singapore to become a completely independent state. At the same period, communist leaders and parties also arose in many areas of Southeast Asia as well, for example, the Malayan Communist Party, the Indonesian Communist Party and the Vietminh in Vietnam to seize back control from their western masters. Historically, nationalism in Thailand has never been as powerful as in its neighbour Vietnam and Cambodia, since it was never colonised. But nationalist sentiments did fuel the military coup in 1932 that overthrew the absolute monarchy.

The former colonies were left with weakly institutionalised political systems that had but a semblance of political–administrative separation or no systems at all following the military coups. In line with the trend towards a state-centric model of development, the public service hence became the main stakeholder in undertaking development initiatives. After obtaining independence, most of these newly independent states began to pursue state-led socioeconomic development and restructure their inherited colonial bureaucracy in favour of development-oriented public administration (Haque, 1996). The emphasis of such a development administration model is on the adoption and implementation of state-led economic plans and programmes through a new set of development-oriented public agencies and officials towards achieving nation-building goals (Haque, 2004). Except for countries such as Vietnam and Cambodia, the administrative systems in Southeast Asia had also evolved in line with the liberal democratic models of public administration characterised by principles such as separation of power, political neutrality and public accountability, which were to be maintained through constitutional provision, legal system, legislative means, ministerial supervision, budget and audit and performance evaluation. This led to the development of an institutionalised government that consists of development planning commissions, boards, councils, agencies to provide efficient administration.

Proceeding from the attainment of self-governance, some of these Southeast Asian nations, particularly Malaysia and Singapore, reoriented their acquired colonial bureaucracy towards a developmental style of governance (Haque, 2006) while others, like Cambodia, struggled to expand their civil service due to volatile local climates. As manifested in Malaysia and Singapore and elaborated below, the developmental administrative approach encompasses a state-centric paradigm where nations developed their own set of programmes, policies and public agencies to aid their pursuit of socioeconomic and political developmental goals (Haque, 2007). Through the lens of talent management, this brand of governance results in the recruitment of a specific type of personnel or the application of distinctive human resource policies to acquaint existing public servants with the nation's new ideology. Thailand among the Southeast Asian nations had never been colonised by European powers. Thai 'independence' was purchased with acceptance of unequal treaties with French and British imperial powers, in which not only land was ceded but extraterritoriality was granted not only to the Europeans but also to colonised Asian subjects of the European powers (Chua, 2008).

Following independence from the French colonial rule, the Kingdom of Cambodia resumed its rule from 1953 to 1970. During this period, moderate improvements were made to the bureaucracy. One particular enhancement concerned the management of the Khum. The head of the commune (Mekhum) was now selected through the general, direct and secret ballots system. These chiefs had two purposes to fulfil: to represent the central government in enforcing laws and regulations and to represent the Khum. They also had a number of responsibilities besides collecting taxes such as looking into the local education and public health matters and allocating lands to farmers (Prum, 2005). Another enhancement was the creation of a public administrative statute called the kram in 1953 where civil servants were employed through the use of competition and were further ranked into four distinctive grades with varying advantages (Vandeluxe, 2014).

New public management: market-driven state policies and business-like restructuring of public sector

Many countries in Southeast Asia were largely influenced by the bureaucratic western models and liberal democratic values in developed nations (Haque, 1996). Bureaucracies were also deemed to be key to developmental effectiveness. From the late 20th to the 21st century, governments in Southeast Asia began to adopt a business-like model of administration according to the 'New Public Management' (NPM) theory. This form of governance encapsulates the ambit of administrative modifications where techniques, strategies and axioms usually harnessed by the private sector, such as performance management metrics and contracting out service provisions, are co-opted by public agencies to improve their efficiency, productivity and adaptability (Samaratunge et al., 2008; Robinson, 2015).

Employing NPM in talent strategies is particularly important for the public service as this would empower them to secure essential talents to sufficiently address the unprecedented challenges of the future. With the proliferation of market-driven state policies and the business-like restructuring of public service, the patterns of administrative ethics have changed in developed nations themselves. There is an increasing priority of pro-market values or business norms which include efficiency, competition, value-for-money, entrepreneurship and partnership which had also impacted on talent management strategies in the public sector.

Taking inspiration from the global movement towards managerialism and pro-market ideals, the governments have implemented a variety of administrative reforms to streamline the roles and management of the public sector. In the lens of human resource management, these reforms were meant to improve the efficiency of the bureaucracy, eliminate unnecessary processes and make sure that the size of the civil service is proportionate with its revised responsibilities. One such reform was the downscaling of the enormous bureaucracy through various measures such as limiting the creation of new positions, getting rid of unoccupied positions in noncritical areas, evaluating job placements in statutory boards, fusing some state services into the federal civil services and privatising government projects, amongst others (Siddiquee, 2006).

Civil service reform in Singapore, Malaysia, Thailand, Cambodia and Vietnam

From colonisation to independence to state-driven development, the region's social, economic, infrastructure and political (both domestic and regional) developments is also witnessed in the reform of each of the country's civil service (Pollitt, 2009). We will briefly look at the reforms in the public sector particularly highlighting the unique features of the civil service in Singapore, Malaysia, Thailand, Cambodia, Myanmar and Vietnam. It is imperative that the administrative metamorphoses do not occur at the same time across all nations as the strategies are designed to cater to each developmental stage of the respective country.

Singapore

Singapore had rapidly transformed from being a low-income country postindependence to a high-income country (World Bank, 2019). It is the only country which has attained the 'developed' status in the Southeast Asia region. The government and the public sector have played an important role in its success and transformation. Singapore has always been a part of

Malaysia until it achieved independence in 1965. During the British's colonisation, it was utilised as a base for the coloniser's expeditions. As such, the most elementary administrative structure and a small bureaucracy were instituted to enable Britain to focus solely on fostering economic activities while ensuring that minimal costs were incurred to maintain Singapore (Low, 2018). Even so, the local colonial bureaucracy was disengaged from the locals, and hiring practices were biased. Senior positions were reserved for the 'natural-born British subjects of pure European descent on both sides' while the Singapore citizens were employed into rank-and-file positions such as policemen and clerks. Even when tertiary-educated locals were accepted into the higher civil service placements, their work stipulations were disproportionate to those of their European counterparts (Low, 2016).

When Singapore's People's Action Party (PAP) government assumed office in 1959 after obtaining independence from British rule, extensive reforms were carried out in the inherited colonial bureaucracy to ensure that the nation's socioeconomic developmental programmes could be effectively implemented. The system of government, however, is still modelled after the Westminster parliamentary model with three separate branches, i.e., the Legislature (comprises the President and Parliament), the Executive (comprises cabinet ministers and office-holders, led by the Prime Minister) and the Judiciary (Parliament of Singapore, 2020). As part of its transformation, Singapore Civil Service's workload was reduced to enhance its competency and statutory boards were created to absorb a portion of that work and execute the various socioeconomic policies in the nation. Statutory boards are an important part of the Singapore public sector. They are separate from the civil service and are operationally autonomous government corporations, governed by a board of directors appointed by the government (Quah, 2010a). They are responsible for specialist, professional and technical services, regulation of businesses and infrastructure operators, land allocations and various forms of control and licensing (Jones, 2018; Saxena, 2011). Government-linked companies (GLCs) are also another group of key entities in which the government holds an exclusive or majority stake through Temasek Holdings, responsible for the state's industrial and infrastructure development.

An attitudinal reform was also put in place to convince existing civil servants to participate in the process of achieving national development. While the British Civil Service was based on the doctrine of political neutrality, the PAP believed that 'the values of the civil servants were irrelevant, if not dysfunctional in the context of mass politics' (Seah, 1971). Some major initiatives were launched to change the values of the current civil servants. This included a Political Study Centre to offer part-time courses to civil servants; reducing civil servants' allowances; recruiting Chinese-educated graduates to dilute the dominance of the English-educated officers; and implementing a policy of selective retention and retirement of the existing senior public officials.

Meritocratic-based criterion was emphasised for the recruitment and promotion in the move away from the patronage and seniority-based system (Quah, 2010b; Quah, 1996). Institutional reform was also enacted to prevent corruption, which was rampant at that time, through the strengthening of existing legislation, such as the amendment of the 1937 Prevention of Corruption Ordinance in 1960, creating a public investigative agency – the Corrupt Practices Investigation Bureau in 1952 – and increasing penalties for such unethical behaviours. In 1972 and in subsequent years such as 1979, 1982 and 1989, the salaries and working conditions for civil servants were improved to remove any form of temptation that can lead to corrupt activities, to minimise the brain drain of senior public officials, and to attract and retain talented individuals in the SCS (Quah, 1996; Quah, 2010c).

In the modern era of new public management as the state adopted enterprise-like management styles, new institutions and statutory boards were established to oversee the public service personnel and enact new human resource policies effectively. One such institution is the Public Service Division (PSD) that was inaugurated in 1983 to take over some of the talent management operations previously undertaken by the PSC, such as workforce development and personnel employment (Public Service Division [PSD], 2015; PSD, 2020). This transfer of responsibilities freed up the PSC to exclusively concentrate on the critical aspects of the SCS, particularly, managing appointments to the senior management ranks and maintaining discipline of the bureaucracy (Public Service Commission, 2019). Another institution that was created to enhance civil servants' spoken and management competencies was the Staff Training Institute in 1971 (known as Civil Service College today) through running a well-designed and coherent milestone-based training curriculum (PSD, 2015). Reflecting the influence of the meritocratic system, membership of the administrative service is reserved for the so-called 'brightest and best'. The talent schemes and leadership development strategies are also designed on the basis of the principle of meritocracy.

Malaysia

Like Singapore, Malaysia inherited from the British a system of Parliamentary Democracy with a bicameral legislature based on the Westminster system through the 1957 Reid Commission (Fernando, 2019; Fernando &

Rajagopal, 2017). While Singapore and Malaysia may be geographical neighbours, their paths to development have not always been the same. Since achieving Independence from Britain in 1957, the Malaysian economy has been structurally reformed through the move from a heavy reliance on raw materials such as rubber and tin to an industrial-based situation. Most of these changes and especially the development of heavy industries had been aided by government-funded agencies. This placed a heavy economic burden on the State. Unlike Singapore's economy which is highly state-driven, the high dependence on the private sector as the main economic driver in Malaysia reduced government involvement in the economy.

In Malaysia, as Malays were economically lagging behind the non-Malay groups (such as the Chinese and Indians) and facing an armed insurrection by an ethnic Chinese communist party, preferential treatment of the Malay race was practised in the civil service as well as in many of the policies (Lim, 2007). A quota system of four Malay employees to one Non-Malay employee was implemented by the British High Commissioner. After independence, the special rights of the Malays (from henceforth will be referred to as the 'bumiputras') were recognised and guaranteed in the 1957 Federal Constitution (Chin, 2011; Tilman, 1961). Such ethnic quota system in managing the employment of the bumiputras and non-bumiputras into the public service continue to be in practice today to ensure Malay's domination of the public service, which was key to boosting their political power and improving their economic condition. For instance, the Malaysian Administrative and Diplomatic Service (Perkhimatan Tadbir dan Diplomatik (PTD)), an elite public agency, implemented the 4:1 quota, and other senior services such as the police, judicial and legal services applied the 3:1 quota in favour of the bumiputras (Chin, 2011). By 1970, the ratio of bumiputras to non-bumiputras had increased to 6:1 (Chin, 2011; Lim, 2007).

Malay control of the bureaucracy became part of the ruling ideology by the incumbent United Malays National Organization (UMNO) party and this was obtained through occupying senior positions, or positions with critical decision-making clout, in all government and government-controlled bodies, with Malays. This preferential treatment of employing and promoting Malays over the talented and skilled non-Malays in the public sector inhibited the government's policy responsiveness towards the non-bumiputras and further diminished the administration's efficiency to meet the needs of all ethnic groups within the populace (Lim, 2007). Under the political leadership of Tun Mahathir Mohamed, the reform agenda was enhanced to accelerate ethnic Malays' participation in the economy and public administration through all policies in addition to the new economic policy (NEP). This included the privatisation of state enterprises.

Many plans and policies were introduced and refined over time in light of modernisation, including demands of better governance and performance management reforms over each leadership change with emphasis on industrialisation and export orientation (Beh, 2018).

A confluence of forces and challenges on the global and domestic fronts such as the universal undertaking of the adoption of NPM values and the local effects of substantial operational costs, large deficiencies and huge bureaucracies on the country provided the impetus for the Malaysian government to renovate the existing government apparatus to one that is more 'hands-off', efficient, dynamic, customer-oriented and market-driven (Siddiquee, 2006). Taking inspiration from the global movement towards managerialism and pro-market ideals, the Malaysian government subsequently implemented a variety of administrative reforms to streamline the roles and management of the public sector. One such reform was the downscaling of the nation's enormous bureaucracy through various measures such as limiting the creation of new positions, getting rid of unoccupied positions in non-critical areas, evaluating job placements in statutory boards, fusing some state services into the federal civil services and privatising government projects, amongst others (Siddiquee, 2006).

While the country has enacted diverse reformations and innovative practices to improve its human resource management in the public sector, limited impacts have resulted. The bureaucracy's performances and provision of public services have been unpromising, incidents of corruption and cronyism persist, errant public servants are not disciplined sufficiently and human capital development improves at a slow pace, amongst others (Siddiquee, 2006). Coupled with the long-standing bumiputra policies, these challenges have and continue to hinder the development of the public service.

Thailand

Thailand remained as an independent kingdom and constitutional monarchy with the military and the religion of Buddhism involved in the shaping of Thai society and politics (Yavaprabhas, 2018). Although it was never colonised, its administrative system had also evolved towards the western bureaucratic style under the regime of King Chulalongkorn. These reforms based on the western model of administration included uniform standards of public service, arrangement of career services, the principle of neutral politics and separation between public office and personal life.

The first Civil Service Act of 1928 was enacted to introduce a merit system based on competence, equity, security and political neutrality (OCSC, 1993). This signified a change from absolute monarchy to democracy in

1932 to shift power from the royal family to the bureaucrats, including the military officers. Since 1932, when the country became a constitutional democracy, administrative power was mainly in the hands of military dictators and the monarchy with a weak and unstable political system. Therefore, the civil servants were able to resist reforms and only minor adjustments were made to the existing structure and practices (Painter, 2004). The government of Thailand increasingly pursued an interventionist developmental role through the creation of many state enterprises. During the 1960s and 1970s, there emerged a stronger alliance between the state and the private sector, the political and administrative elites assumed greater power in the name of enhancing the nation's development agenda [44]. The Thai government established the National Institute of Development Administration (NIDA) in 1966 under the ministry of education in order to provide education and training in development-related public administration. In the 1970s, the new curriculum of NIDA put greater emphasis on economic development and development administration [45].

Major changes in the Thai public sector only happened from 1991 during the military coup which followed with the establishment of a national legislature that turned state power from the hands of politicians to public bureaucrats (Yavaprabhas, 2018). In 1997, the 'People's constitution' was drafted and approved by the National Assembly which comprises 99 members of which 76 of them were directly elected from each of the provinces and the rest 23 were qualified persons being shortlisted mainly from academia and other sectors. The new constitution contains several initiatives such as reform of the legislative system, an election reform, a mechanism to strengthen the executive branch, separation between the executive and legislation branches, an increased check and balance system, an explicit recognition of human rights, a clear separation of the judicial system from the executive branch, establishment of accountability institutions as constitution-independent organisations. It also provides methods for increasing citizen participation and enhancing transparency and accountability as well as decentralisation. It promulgates new standards for transparency and guidelines for decentralising authority and resources to local administrations.

With subsequent street protests, riots following corruption accusations of the governments, critical reforms in the Thai public sector were initiated to decentralise power from the national government to localities and creation of new forms of the public administration organisations similar to Quasi Non-Governmental Organisations (QUANGOs) as well as to grant more autonomy to the local government. The Office of Civil Service Commission was also established to oversee the development and performance of the civil service.

Cambodia

Compared to Singapore, Malaysia and Thailand, Cambodia did not have the opportunity and time to develop its bureaucracy to enable the attainment of socioeconomic and political development goals due to regime changes occurring across a period of nearly four decades. At each chapter of regime change, the Cambodian public service suffered setbacks in its own development as it succumbed to the prevailing political ideologies at each time. For instance, during the radical rule of the Khmer Rouge, all administrative institutions and public servants were destroyed. When a new Cambodian government was set up under a Vietnamese leadership, the bureaucracy was characterised by an autocratic centralism creed. Officials were chosen at the district or commune stratums and not at the higher level of administration where the dominating party, the People's Republic of Kampuchea (PRK), ruled. Occurrences of patronage were rampant and the established bureaucracy valued allegiance and acquiescence over performance quality and efficiency (Blunt & Turner, 2005). Following this, the United Nations Transitional Authority in Cambodia (UNTAC) entered the nation with several consultants and military personnel in the hopes of initiating a democratic government. Consequently, the system of governance and bureaucracy that was established was predicated on alien customs and tenets that were influenced by foreign agents. All these fluctuations in political structures and the resulting traumas adversely impacted Cambodia's administrative advancement. Each bureaucracy that was created as part of regime changes was discordant with the needs of the locals and this ultimately resulted in a bureaucracy that had inadequate capabilities in national development (Downie & Kingsbury, 2001).

The development of the nation's economy and civil service only truly began in the recent two decades. This is evident in the various strategies and national agendas that have been legislated to stimulate institutional improvements, economic development and good governance (World Bank Group, 2018). For instance, the initial Rectangular Strategy Phase I in 2004 by the Royal Government of Cambodia is a thorough programme to boost sustainable growth of the nation and diminish poverty through diverse strategies such as augmenting the capacity of public institutions, improving the public sector's efficacy, safeguarding the country's natural assets and producing employment opportunities for citizens. Furthermore, as part of this strategy, the government championed the National Program for Administrative Reform (NPAR) to renovate the civil service by streamlining the bureaucracy, distributing powers to the communes and simplifying the process of public service deliveries (Sen, 2004). In a like manner, subsequent agendas embraced by the government – Rectangular Strategy Phase

II (Sen, 2008), Rectangular Strategy Phase III (Sen, 2013), Rectangular Strategy Phase IV (Sen, 2018) – aim to broaden and expand on the four identified themes of growth, employment, equity and efficiency through continuously building upon past reformations to ultimately catalyse economic advancement that will put the nation in the upper-middle-income category (World Bank Group, 2018).

In terms of improving public administration, the government has chosen to stress on three key components: bolstering the superiority and efficiency of service delivery, enriching human resource development policies through initiatives such as implementing a civil servant performance and accountability scheme and enhancing public servants' ethics and discipline, and reforming the remuneration framework (Sen, 2013; Sok, 2013). Over the years, some of the reforms that have been carried out concerning talent management in the public service include raising the pay and pensions of civil servants from 2013 to 2017 and developing a computerised human resources management information system (HRMIS) that would enable the public sector human resource team to easily manage their payroll and keep track of every public servant's employment history from first posting to retirement. However, as a three-tier administrative system exists in Cambodia, challenges to systematise talent management processes linger throughout the nation. One such challenge is the underutilisation of the HRMIS system at the subnational level. Data on public servants are still submitted in paper format to the Ministry of Civil Service (MCS) resulting in a duplication of data at the hiring ministry and MCS levels (World Bank Group, 2018). Given the complicated arrangement of the country, Cambodia still has a long way to go to achieve a high level of consistency and harmonisation of human resource policies within its public administration.

Vietnam

The trajectory of public administration reforms in Vietnam can be discerned to have triggered a change in the decision-making processes, accountability and public service delivery on the national and global fronts. Prior to independence, the local system of administration had been typified by the principles of hierarchy where the lower levels of government were subjected to the higher levels and collective leadership where the majority vote dictated outcomes. The impetus provided by the country's economic development and liberalisation from a centrally planned unit to an open and market-oriented system to one that is entrenched in a regional and global integration has resulted in the country's public administration reformations correspondingly transitioning from improving and strengthening the state apparatus, tackled by the 'Doi Moi' renovation programme, to confronting new emerging challenges and meeting citizens' demands for a more transparent and responsible government with an enhanced public service performance and delivery (Pham, 2018).

Under the 'Doi Moi' renovation programme from 1986 to 1999, renovations in Vietnam's public administration permeated from the central to the local levels of government where initiatives such as improving the law-making process, trimming the bureaucracy size, combating corruption and promoting the personal responsibilities and authority of senior officials were implemented. This administrative transformation brought to light a new set of obstacles thereby necessitating an unfaltering and comprehensive public administration reformation framework. Consequently, the 9th and 11th Party Congress developed the Master programme on Public Administration Reform (PAR) for the two-decade periods of 2001–2010 and 2011–2020.

Some of the administrative issues that the two Master programmes on PAR aimed at mitigating were: (a) the absence of a professional civil service due to causes such as an unclear distinction among officials employed in the state and party organs, the immanent occurrence of 'cadre transfers' within the political body and the incapability of the government to preserve a group of qualified civil servants; (b) the feeble, uncompromising and unaccommodating government institutions and mechanisms that were antithetical to the market economy; (c) the presence of bribery and corruption among civil servants; and (d) the stipulations for obligated administration reforms due to Vietnam's membership in regional and international cooperative bodies such as ASEAN and the WTO. These challenges have prompted the government to implement multiple administrative renovations, including the adoption of new civil service regulations and updating the civil service salary scheme to be on par with market rates in ensuring civil service professionalism, decentralising the decision-making process and delineating public officials' work procedures, functions and duties as part of an organisational reform, instituting anti-corruption agencies throughout all levels of government to address public service misconduct and the application of international best practices in public administration such as embracing the new public management (NPM) ideology and internationally certified standards (ISO) accreditation to parallel the public service governance of regional and international nations and strengthen local service delivery and performance.

Even as these public administration reforms that have been enacted in Vietnam are ambitious, and in some cases successful in reforming service delivery, they have nonetheless unearthed key shortcomings that stand in the way of a total and complete administrative overhaul. Some of these prevalent fault lines are the absence of a systematic and consistent regulatory system and a continued paucity in civil service professionalism. To ensure that the nation's numerous public administration reforms achieve their desired outcomes and to assuage the frustrations of local and international stakeholders, a concerted and robust effort among the nation's leaders from the top to the grassroots levels is thereby essential.

Sustaining administrative reforms through talent management and leadership development

Public sector reforms, even not implemented government-wide, involve fundamental changes in structure and processes that require new policies, legal or legislative actions. These reforms often aligned with the developmental stages of the countries and towards achieving their socioeconomic goals, usually triggered by political agenda. In Southeast Asia, the emergence of state-driven public administration coincided with the region's economic growth and industrial progress since the post-colonisation period to date. The public sector hence played a significant role in accelerating economic growth, developing infrastructure and public services, and upgrading the living standards of citizens. Even though the countries are at differing level of development, with Singapore being the most developed while Cambodia being the least developed with different priorities ranging from solving corruption to industrialisation to digitisation, it is vital for governments to build a pool of educated and trained public servants with the necessary skillsets and abilities across the various government organisations to successfully implement policies and carry out initiatives at the various levels.

2 Talent management as a growing discipline in the public sector

Defining talent management in the public sector

Talent management (TM) as a growing discipline has given rise to three significant themes. Firstly, there is the discussion of exclusive or inclusive TM approaches (Dries, 2013). This debate concentrates on whether TM activities should focus on all employees (Ingham, 2006) or only on those select few identified as talent (Lewis & Heckman, 2006). The second theme concerns the intended employee outcomes of TM with the implicit assumption of the 'Pygmalion effect' (Eden, 1984). The Pygmalion effect occurs when others' expectations of high performance (e.g., from the talent's supervisor) positively influence the actual/perceived performance of talents (Dries, 2013; Gallardo-Gallardo et al., 2013). Research on employee reactions to talent identification reports positive effects for talents on attitudinal outcomes, such as commitment to increased performance demands, building skills and supporting strategic priorities (Björkman et al., 2013). It purports that those who are excluded from the talent pool experience career disadvantages. It suggests that those who are identified as a talent experience more positive outcomes than those who are not identified as a talent. The third theme critically addresses the conflation of TM practices and activities promoted by consultancy firms and practitioner associations (Stahl et al., 2012; Swailes, 2013). This implied that TM practices are implicitly based on 'unitarist' or 'top-to-down' approach assume mutual gains for both the employer and employee but with little focus being given to employee voice (Movius & Susskind, 2009; Thunnissen et al., 2013). Out of the three themes, the first theme on TM practices within the spectrum of inclusivity–exclusivity pertains more to the public sector. This is due to the unique characteristics of the public sector and the limited resource and budget allocation.

Talent management has been a topic of interest for managers and HR practitioners for many years. But finding a clear definition is difficult. The Chartered Institute for Personnel and Development (CIPD) defines talent management as: '. . . *the systematic attraction, identification, development, engagement, retention and deployment of those individuals who are of particular value to an organisation, either in view of their "high potential" for the future or because they are fulfilling business/operation-critical roles'* (CIPD, 2016). Generally, the three main processes of TM are '*attract, develop and retain*'. The plethora of definitions and the breadth of the CIPD definition highlight the complexity of talent management which requires a collaborative relationship between the employee and the organisation. Despite the challenges, talent management is being embraced in all sectors including the public sector. Some examples of the frameworks used to study talent management include the competency approach adopted to study senior public service leaders (Bhatta, 2001; Mau, 2009); self-selection approach (Delfgaauw & Dur, 2010); and the talent management approach (Frank & Taylor, 2004; Lewis & Heckman, 2006). The majority of publications on TM in the public sector do not offer a formal definition of their central concept (Dries, 2013) and the approaches to conceptualisations of talent and TM that are being put forth in academic literature today differ significantly from each other (Armstrong, 2007; Gallardo-Gallardo et al., 2013; Thunnissen et al., 2013). Textbooks on TM in general – for example, Cappelli (2008) and Berger and Berger (2010) – do not explicitly cover the public sector, while textbooks on public sector human resource management – for example, Berman et al. (2009) and Pynes (2009) – do not adequately discuss talent strategies and surrounding issues. The scant literature mostly focused on TM in specific public or nonprofit organisations such as health care, and education institutes – for example, Davies and Davies (2010), Groves (2011), Powell et al. (2012), Van den Brink et al. (2013) – and specific practices and approaches in the countries – for example, Kim and Scullion (2011), Poocharoen and Lee (2013), Buttiens and Hondeghem (2015) and Thunnissen and Buttiens (2017).

Moreover, empirical studies on TM in the public sector have also been limited to surveys of what is done in practice. For example, Pollitt and Bouckaert (2004) studied how the top civil servants and 'high fliers' of seven European countries were trained. The Cornerstone OnDemand study of the US civil service approach identifies a number of talent management practices common to all levels of US government service which highlights the weaknesses of the US government agencies lagging in managing talents (Cornerstone, 2009). Most studies have focused on single-country cases. For example, Duggett (2001) studied four decades of the British civil service training institute and its priorities; Bhatnagar (2007) studied talent management in an Indian public agency; and Macfarlane's study in 2012 showed that TM in the UK National Health Service is rationalistic, bureaucratic, centralised, standardised and performance managed. However, these studies did not take into consideration the organisational context. Considering that the preference of an organisation for a certain aspect of talent management can be placed within the contingency or best-fit model (Garrow & Hirsh, 2008; Vaiman & Collings, 2013), studies were conducted via in-depth interviews and Poocharoen and Lee's (2013) study of TM schemes in the three countries identified structure and scope of authority of the responsible agencies, flexibility of incentives and that differing performance appraisal systems can lead to varying TM practices. Buttiens and Hondeghem's (2015) research on talent management in the Flemish government presented an overall picture of the specific approaches, goals and human resources (HR) processes of talent management in a public-sector context, which is primarily influenced by the social/cultural/legal dimensions by considering the viewpoints of various stakeholders. Most recently, Thunnissen and Buttiens (2017) clarified how public-sector organisations conceptualise TM especially with regard to what contextual factors influence the adoption of an inclusive or a more segmented approach when identifying talents in the public sector.

This points to specific tensions that may arise in the process of implementing talent management practices within well-embedded organisational approaches to equality and diversity in public-sector organisations (Harris & Foster, 2010). Dries' (2013) review of TM resulted in the identification of five tensions regarding the operationalisation of talent, namely: inclusive versus exclusive, objective versus subject, innate versus acquired, input versus output, and transferable versus context dependent. The study also reflects differences in the meaning of 'talent' across different cultures, that is, the Anglo-American stance of positioning talent as relatively high performance may not be shared in cultures that are more collective and less performance oriented. Developing from this, Boselie and Thunnissen's (2017) chapter on talent management in the public sector discusses further the tensions and dualities regarding TM in the public sector due to conflicting interests and outcomes of stakeholders by adopting a multidisciplinary approach to talent management, using human resource management, public administration and public management. Later studies that look into inclusive or exclusive approaches to defining talents – for example, in Meyers' 'Talent management: Towards a more inclusive understanding' (2016) – also suggest a trend towards a more inclusive approach to address overall talent scarcity and hard-to-predict market dynamics. Buttiens and Hondeghem's (2015) study of the Flemish public sector also concluded that the inclusive approach to talent management is the prevalent approach.

Tension between inclusive and exclusive perspectives on talent

As defining talent tends to evoke the tension between the inclusiveness or exclusiveness of the TM practices in the public sector, and later studies

(Buttiens & Hondeghem, 2015; Meyers, 2016; Thunnissen & Buttiens, 2017; Kravariti & Johnston, 2020) also point to the prevalent tension between inclusive and exclusive approaches in the public sector, we will only focus on this. To understand TM in the public sector, we first need to define 'talent'. Talent can be defined as an innate and integral component of intelligence or *'the sum of a person's abilities . . . his or her intrinsic gifts, skills, knowledge, experience, intelligence, judgement, attitude, character, and drive'*. It also includes his or her ability to 'learn and grow' (Michaels et al., 2001). Talent is also shaped as an idea of aptitude, mastery, commitment and fit, obviously innate ability, skills, knowledge and attitudes which will achieve better performances (Gallardo-Gallardo et al., 2013). Ulrich takes a more holistic view to define talent as a combination of competence, commitment and contribution (2006). In a report by the Chartered Institute of Personnel and Development (CIPD, 2016) on the future of talent in Singapore 2030, the term 'talent' was explored extensively and the high-level conceptual definition that was proposed revolved around the themes of the ability: to learn, evolve and adapt; to create and innovate; and to deliver excellent results in the present and potential for future performance. This implies that talented individuals will learn and understand at a faster rate within the domain of their talent than their non-talented peers. However, Meyers et al. (2013) also indicated that though innate talent may be a necessary (but not a sufficient) condition for reaching exceptional performance levels, it must be coupled with training, development and experiences. Therefore, deliberate practice and skill are the foremost important predictors of performance (Meyers et al., 2013). Similarly, experience was indispensable for attaining the required competencies that qualify a future leader (McCall, 1998). With regard to this, it is suggested that talented individuals possess a particular set of characteristics such as proactively finding new learning experiences; comprehensive understanding of management; considering problems from new perspectives, taking risks, seeking feedback, learning from mistakes etc. (McCall, 1998). Tansley (2011) defines talent as a high potential employee who has the ability, engagement and aspiration to rise to and reach more senior, more critical positions while successful performance also can be linked to other characteristics most often related to talented individuals, such as high levels of experience, leadership behaviours, creativity and initiative stemming from a ''can-do attitude'. In which, the individual potential is decided by the three factors namely: above-average ability; high task commitment; and high creativity as latent factor that influences future development and success (Yost & Chang, 2009). Table 2.1 summarises the different relevant definitions of talent from the literature surveyed.

Table 2.1 Definitions of talent (reproduced from Lee & Rezaei, 2019)

References	Suggested Definition of Talent
Michaels et al. (2001)	Talent is the sum of a person's abilities – his or her intrinsic gifts, skills, knowledge, experience, intelligence, judgement, attitude, character and drive. It also includes his or her ability to learn and grow
Tansley et al. (2006)	Talent can be considered as a complex amalgam of employees' skills, knowledge, cognitive ability and potential. Employees' values and work preferences are also of major importance
Tansley et al. (2007)	Talent consists of those individuals who can make a difference to organisational performance, either through their immediate contribution or in the longer term by demonstrating the highest levels of potential
Tansley (2011)	Talent tends to be specific to an organisation and highly influenced by the nature of the work undertaken. Therefore, a shared organisational language for talent is important
Ulrich and Smallwood (2012)	'Talent = competence [knowledge, skills and values required for today's and tomorrow's job; right skills, right place, right job, right time] × commitment [willing to do the job] × contribution [finding meaning and purpose in their job]' (p. 60)
CIPD (2012)	Talents refer to individuals with high potential who are of particular value to an organisation either in view of their 'high potential' for the future or because they are fulfilling business/operation-critical roles
Lee and Rezaei (2019); Poocharoen and Lee (2013); Swailes and Blackburn (2016)	Talent refers to the exclusive elite/specialised individuals versus the inclusive whole of the workforce
Dries (2013); Boselie and Thunnissen (2017)	Talent can be constructed as capital, as giftedness, as identity and individual strength, differentiating individuals of high value to organisations or individuals with high potential and materially shapes practices in people management

In relevance to these definitions and attributes to talent, there are generally two dimensions to categorise talent, yielding four typologies of talent. The primary dimension classifies talent as either subjects (people) or objects (characteristics of people). The second views talent as an exclusive labour resource (group) or an inclusive workforce (all employees). In general, there are two approaches. First, there is the exclusive perspective whereby some people are deemed to be more talented than others, while for the inclusive perspective one starts from the premise that all employees are talented.

In the exclusive perspective, the 'talented people' group are defined as people with high potential and high performance, creating unique values, unique strengths for the organisation, who are able to create significant differences in the organisation's activities at present or in the future (Von Seldeneck, 2004). Based on these concepts, talent can be seen as an individual or a group of persons who possess outstanding qualifications and abilities, exceptional achievements and influences on the overall progress and development of the organisation. The levels of performance required from individual talent will naturally depend on the needs of the organisation and the nature of the work (Tansley, 2011). From this point, the organisations should have a clear view of what kind of talent that they need, based on the needs and missions of organisations. The 'exclusive' or 'elite high-potential' mode of talent management is 'characterized by a concentration of those in the one or two segments (or talent "pools") of the workforce who are either at the top or who are identified as having the potential to get to the top by demonstrating high levels of potential or performance' (Tansley et al., 2006). These top-level employees are the 'best and brightest'. Conversely, the 'inclusive' or 'whole workforce' approach 'recognizes that there are various key positions to fill in any organisation as well as future pipelines for the appropriate skills to fill all these positions' (Tansley et al., 2006, p. 3). Inclusive talent perspective is deeply grounded in the assumption that all employees have valuable qualities or talents that can be productively applied in organisations. This is one of the key propositions of positive psychology, that focuses on all aspects of life that are good or well-functioning (Seligman & Csikszentmihalyi, 2000). Hence, inclusive talent management undergirds 'the recognition and acceptance that all employees have talent together with the ongoing evaluation and deployment of employees in positions that give the best fit and opportunity (via participation) for employees to use those talents' (Swailes et al., 2014, p. 5). Such an approach aims to bring out the best in all employees, allowing all employees to realise their full potential at work.

Definition of talent shaping the talent management strategy

Consequently, depending on the position an organisation is taking on the inclusive–exclusive continuum, the talent management policy of an organisation will be shaped on the basis of either an exclusive mode which focused on a specific group of talents or a more inclusive mode that encompasses all employees in the organisation, and materially shapes practices in people management (Dries, 2013; Nijs, 2014; Boselie & Thunnissen, 2017). Concentrating merely on key strategic positions or those groups of employees that occupy these strategic positions can be considered as a one-dimensional focus on organisational goals. Incorporation of an inclusivity-oriented talent management approach in the personnel policy of an organisation, however, makes it possible to acquire a multidimensional view on performance (the individual and societal level as well as the economic goals of the organisation) and hence acknowledge that everyone possesses strengths and competencies. This also means that it aims at investing in a broad variety of different talents. Having said that, it is important to note that inclusive talent management acknowledges the possibility that employees possess talents that do not fit a particular organisation. In these cases, organisations should provide assistance to employees to find more suitable employment elsewhere (Swailes et al., 2014) so that their talents do not go to waste.

All these can be encapsulated to define TM as 'the systematic attraction, identification, development, engagement/retention, and deployment of those individuals with high potential who are of particular value to an organization, either in view of their "high potential" for the future or because they are fulfilling business/operation-critical roles' (CIPD, 2012). The plethora of definitions and the breadth of the CIPD's (2012) definition reflects one of the most central debates in TM, that is, whether TM is an inclusive approach that focuses on the talents and abilities of all employees or an exclusive approach focused on attracting, developing, rewarding and retaining a specific group of employees (Tansley, 2011; Dries, 2013; Gallardo-Gallardo et al., 2013; Poocharoen & Lee, 2013; Boselie & Thunnissen, 2017. This leads to a tension between definitions of talent as high-potential versus high-performance individuals (Thunnissen et al., 2013; Collings, 2014; Boselie & Thunnissen, 2017) particularly in the public sector whereby performance is a diffuse construct (Ulrich & Ulrich, 2010) and public service and public value are often not offered alone but are rather the result of a team effort (Boselie & Thunnissen, 2017).

In the public sector, the definition of talent seems to shift towards the exclusive approach and the conceptualisation of talent is highly influenced by the tension between equality and differentiation. Employee differentiation is a key feature in the exclusive approach that is against the principle that all employees should be treated equally and given equal opportunities in the inclusive approach. In the exclusive talent management approach, there is a strict distinction between talent and non-talent; however, it is not clear on what basis the distinction is made (Dries, 2013; Boselie & Thunnissen, 2017), unlike specialists and professionals whereby employee differentiation is generally accepted because of the specific skills and knowledge they possess in addition to recognition by professional institutions. However, when it is applied to functions that are less specialised and more administrative this might cause tensions in the selection of individuals into fast-track talent schemes.

Performance-based reward and promotion to retain young talents

Career development in the public sector is traditionally based on seniority which has led to capable young talents leaving the sector to join the private sector. Therefore, the trend is moving towards appointments with increased emphasis on individual performance. However, it has led to the tension between the measurement of individual and group performances. Performance measurement is defined as the 'quantifying, either quantitatively or qualitatively, the input, output or level of activity of an event or process' (Radnor & Barnes, 2007, p. 393). Previous literature (Pollitt, 2006; Johnsen, 2005; Merchant & Van der Stede, 2003; Modell, 2000; Merchant, 1998; Mol, 1996; Gupta et al., 1994; Hofstede, 1981; Ouchi, 1979, 1980) suggests that outputs are measurable when objectives are clear and unambiguous. If these conditions are not met, reliance on other forms of control is necessary to measure performance for incentive purposes. To some extent, objectives are ambiguous in the public sector. The incidence of political control also increases due to the hierarchical power structures, negotiation processes, particular interests and conflicting agency goals (Vakkuri & Meklin, 2006; Lee, 2018). The success of projects or policies are also not attributable to individual performance, but more of team performance which causes the difficulties of developing fair measurements for individuals. Performance measurement systems provide the basis for the compensation of public government officials especially when new public management models are being adopted and performance management has been integrated into the public sector to enhance the quality of public service. It is noted that careful specification and monitoring of performance, along with a set of incentives can be used to ensure that the motivate public sector managers (Newberry and Pallot, 2004) but due to the characteristics of public sector organisations, it may result in unintended consequences (Pollitt, 2009; Hood and Peters, 2004) and may not be in the best interests of the society. These consequences may include additional internal bureaucracy, a lack of innovation, a lack of transparency, tunnel vision, suboptimisation and gaming to manipulate outputs. Although efforts had been made in the recent decades to move from output/cost-based measurements towards outcome-based measurements (Heinrich, 2002; Borgonovi et al., 2018), but outcome is longer term-based which implicates the assessment of short-term assessment criteria (performance evaluation is on yearly basis). If a person's performance is rated as superior in comparison to his/her past performances rather than between person comparison that will allow individuals to be more energised (Peterson & Seligman, 2004; Quinlan et al., 2012). However, in the context of exclusive talent management approaches, a person is seen as talented only if he or she performs better than the majority of other persons (Gallardo-Gallardo et al., 2013).

Talent scheme as main talent strategy in the public sector

TM programmes or talent schemes are key features of TM practices in the public sector (Poocharoen & Lee, 2013; OECD, 2017; Lee and Rezaei, 2019). Specific recruitment programmes and talent schemes seek to identify the best and brightest for enrolment in higher-intensity development and faster progression schemes (Neo & Chen, 2007; Quah, 2010b; Poocharoen & Lee, 2013; OECD, 2017; Lee & Rezaei, 2019). In a review of talent management practices in OECD countries (OECD, 2017), there were fast-track, high-flyer programmes in 17 countries (e.g., United States' Senior Executive Service, the United Kingdom's Fast Stream, South Korea's Senior Civil Service, Singapore's Administrative Services, Thailand's High Potential Performers and Malaysia's Administrative and Diplomatic schemes). There is great diversity across these programmes, as some focus on bringing new talent while others look within to identify promising individuals for promotion and succession. These programmes are specific public service schemes that adopt an exclusive approach, which implies that a selected few are being identified at an early stage of their career and are groomed further through training and postings to maximise their potential and become future leaders (Dries, 2013; Poocharoen & Lee, 2013; McNulty & Kaveri, 2019). It is implied that talented individuals will learn and understand at a faster rate than their non-talented peers and innate talent may be a necessary condition for reaching exceptional performance levels. However, it is also assumed that the innate talent is not able to attain excellent performances without training, development and experiences; therefore, deliberate courses and projects are provided to expose selected individuals in respective domains. Table 2.2 provides an overview of the size of the public-sector workforce in Singapore, Malaysia, Thailand, Cambodia and Vietnam and summarises the talent management practices in the five countries into the three stages of talent recruitment, development and retention.

Table 2.2 Summary of the public sector and talent management practices in Singapore, Malaysia, Thailand, Cambodia and Vietnam

	Singapore	Malaysia	Thailand	Cambodia	Vietnam
Employment size	About 146,000 officers in 16 ministries and more than 50 statutory boards. Within the public service is the civil service, comprising about 85,000 officers in the ministries in 2020 (PSD, 2020)	1.71 million public servants serving in 36 government agencies and ministries (including local authorities and teachers) as of 2019 (Abas, 2019)	Consists of about 2.19 million personnel, working in 20 ministries and 166 departments. Of these, about one-third are ordinary civil servants under the jurisdiction of the Office of the Civil Service Commission (OCSC) (Yavaprabhas, 2018).	There were over 200,000 civil servants across the country in 2016, including 38,543 national civil servants and 162,475 at subnational levels (Khmer, 2017)	There are 2,726,917 officers working in the public sector. There are 611,069 Public Officials and Civil Servants, 1,983,981 officers working in public service deliveries. (World Bank, 2017)
Central institutions	• Public Service Commission (PSC) • Public Service Division (PSD) • Civil Service College (CSC)	• Jabatan Perkhidmatan Awam (JPA) or Public Service Department • Suruhanjaya Perkhidmatan Awam (SPA) or Public Services Commission • National Institute of Public Administration (INTAN)	• Office of the Civil Service Commission (OCSC) • Office of the Public Sector Development Commission (OPDC) • Civil Service Commission (CSC) • Civil Service Training Institute (CSTI) • King Prajadhipok's Institute (KPI)	• Ministry of Civil Service (MSC) • Royal School of Administration (RSA) • Economics and Finance Institute (EFI)	• Ministry of Home Affairs (MOHA) • Monitoring Office of Programme 165 (MOP 165) • Ho Chi Minh National Academy of Politics and Public Administration (HCMA)

Talent recruitment	Open recruitment (fresh graduates and mid-career entrants) Pre-service bonded scholarships Green harvesting Scouting/head-hunting Transfers between departments/organisations	Open recruitment (fresh graduates and mid-career entrants) Pre-service bonded Scholarships Scouting/head-hunting	Open recruitment (fresh graduates) Pre-service bonded scholarships Public-sector innovation scholarships Public Service Executive Development Programme	Bloc-based recruitment through examinations (fresh graduates and mid-career entrants) Pre-service scholarships (for teachers only) Conversion of contract to permanent staff	Internal recruitment within each ministry and agency (Officials promoted or transferred according to seniority and exam without serious performance evaluation)
Talent development	Allocated training hours Roadmaps for special schemes, i.e., Management Associate Programme (MAP), Administrative Service scheme (AS) Public Sector Leadership programme High potential Bonded in-service scholarships	Allocated training hours Administrative and Diplomatic scheme (PTD) High-performing officer scheme Fast-Track Programme	Allocated training hours High-potential performance system (HiPS) scheme New wave leadership development	Based on selection criteria Relevance to the public finance management, public administration, public decentralisation reforms Career path for Grade A scheme officers (director level to secretary of state)	Training and development to meet the common knowledge required for the experts, principal experts In-service postgraduate scholarships

(Continued)

Table 2.2 (Continued)

	Singapore	Malaysia	Thailand	Cambodia	Vietnam
Talent retention	Competitive pegged-to-market pay structure Performance-based remuneration (salary and bonus) Performance-based promotions High-pay structure for AS	Base pay coupled with types of allowances Both seniority- and performance-based promotions Opportunities for postgraduate studies Fixed pay increment structure	Fast-stream track Performance-based system Higher pay (about 1 per cent for high potentials) Perks in health care and pension schemes	Basic pay sufficient to meet daily needs Set of allowances targeted at priorities (e.g., teachers, senior management) Revision of pay based on reform and Royal Government recommendation Promotions through selection or seniority Bonded scholarships to pursue Ph.D. offered to senior officers (Grade A) supported either by government or development partner	Centralised wage increment Adjustment of pensions, social insurance allowances, prescribed monthly allowances and preferential allowances for officers with meritorious services

3 Talent management and leadership development in Singapore

A meritocratic approach of getting the 'best and brightest'

The country was fraught with economic and social challenges in the early days of independence when it was abruptly forced out of the Federation of Malaysia in 1965. Faced with capital flight, labour strife, communist insurgency, ethnic tensions and high unemployment rate of over 10 per cent (Ngiam and Tay, 2006), the PAP government had to adopt a pragmatic approach towards managing economic and social problems in order to urgently create jobs and meet the housing, education and infrastructure needs of the people. Hence, the economy was almost like a corporate in relentless pursuit of the GDP growth rate and accumulation of reserves. Political office holders and senior civil servants are even remunerated, in part, according to the GDP growth that they deliver, much like corporates reward their senior management with bonuses linked to profits made.

Nurturing people's talents through education is central to the country's economic growth, productivity and development, being beneficial to both its people and society in general (Gopinathan, 2012; Zhao & Wong, 2013). Especially at the heart of the civil service, the spirit of meritocracy sets the main basis for the talent management approach especially at the recruitment stage whereby the 'best and brightest' assessed on the basis of academic achievements are hired (Poocharoen & Lee, 2013). This is based on Singapore's founding father and first prime minister, Lee Kuan Yew's belief that 'If you want Singapore to succeed . . . you must have a system that enables the best man and the most suitable to go into the job that needs them . . .' (Quah, 2010a). Meritocracy offers a fair system, which provides talented and hard-working people from all walks of life with a means of advancement and the opportunity to contribute to the well-being of the larger society. It can be a powerful vehicle for social mobility and incentivise people to do their best and reach their fullest potential.

As the country reached a level of prosperity, stable economic growth and its income per head being one of the highest in the world and achieving a world-class standard of health care, education, housing and infrastructure, there is recognition that its commitment to meritocracy should be integrated with broader social values such as compassion, humility and regard for the poor. The meritocratic approach has often been criticised as a system that breeds elitism due to its over-emphasis on individual effort which can engender a hyper-competitive and individualistic mindset (Young, 1958; Tan, 2008; Tan & Bhaskaran, 2015). Especially after the results from the 2011 general election (GE), however, revealed a growing voice of the public, wanting their needs to be addressed which led to the incumbent PAP receiving the lowest-ever electoral results and face an unprecedented outpouring of discontentment towards rising housing prices and the influx of migrants (Guo & Phua, 2014; Lee et al., 2017). In the attempt to win back votes from those who felt left out and rebuild the legitimacy of its regime, the PAP government for the first time shifted away from the pragmatic approach to consult and engage the public to promote co-creation and coproduction in policy design and service delivery, making policymaking change from top-down mandate to bottom-up collaboration (Lee et al., 2017). Post-NPM approaches, such as 'joined-up government' and 'whole-of-government' programmes, have also been adopted to build collaborative ICT environments in government by the hierarchical strengthening of the centre (Klievink & Janssen, 2009; Ojo et al., 2011). This prompted a mindset change in the government and consequently in its leadership development strategy in the public sector to move away from its elitist exclusive approach.

The Singapore public service

The Public Service employs around 146,000 officers in 16 Ministries and more than 60 Statutory Boards. Within the Public Service is the Civil Service, comprising about 85,000 officers in the Ministries (PSD, 2021). The work scope is broadly categorised into five sectors as follow:

- Central Administration: Strengthening the core of the Singapore Public Service
- Security: Keeping Singapore safe, secure and influential
- Social: Growing the heart-ware of the society
- Infrastructure & Environment: Making the city-state a place to live in
- Economy: Driving our economy

The three agencies that oversee the talent management schemes, policies and its implementation in the public service of Singapore are namely: Public

Service Commission (PSC), Public Service Division (PSD) and the Civil Service College (CSC). PSC as a neutral and independent body safeguards the fundamental principles of integrity, impartiality and meritocracy in the Singapore Public Service. Its key responsibilities include selecting and developing PSC Scholarship holders, appointing Administrative Officers and promoting top talent, maintaining discipline amongst civil servants, and acting as the final appellate board to ensure that all officers are fairly and consistently treated (PSC, 2019). PSD oversees the human resource needs and policies of all public service officers. Moving away from its role as a human resource management regulator in the public service, it has now become a partner with public agencies to attract, develop, retain and engage these officers. Their primary purpose is to oversee the health, well-being, performance, motivation and ethos of the Public Service. PSD put in place individual development plans and work with agencies and training institutes to develop engineering and service delivery capabilities (PSD, 2020). The Civil Service College is a statutory board under the PSD and is the main training institute for the Singapore Public Service to deepen public officers' knowledge and capabilities, strengthen their understanding and empathy for the needs of our citizens, and reinforce their values and commitment to excellence (CSC, 2020).

Pre-service scholarships

The war for talent in the Singapore public service faces tough competition from the higher-paying private sector. The Singapore government believes that offering pre-service scholarships is the best way to attract the 'best and brightest' young men and women to serve the government especially (Quah, 2010b). Therefore, pre-service scholarship schemes are the main talent attraction strategies. There is a diverse range of courses and universities for sponsored study and recipients upon completion of their studies, they will serve through one of three career paths: Public Administration, Professional Service or Uniformed Services (PSC, 2019). Candidates must be Singaporean citizens or Permanent Residents who are keen to take up Singapore citizenship and are assessed primarily on the basis of their high school academic results and Co-Curricular Activities (CCA) records; leadership potential and the desire to serve the public (Poocharoen & Lee, 2013). The candidates must go through a few rounds of interviews and psychometric tests administered mainly by the PSC. Scholars will serve a five- to seven-year bond to the government upon return. In line with the strategic developments of the state, the PSC scholarships had also been changed to offer more specialised domains in 2017 such as in engineering and medicine and dentistry in partnership with the Ministry of Health. The various types of scholarships are summarised in Table 3.1.

Table 3.1 Summary of scholarships offered and administered by the Public Service Commission (PSC)

Scholarship	Domains	Career Pathway	Work Scope	Bond Period
PSC Scholarship	Various (as approved by the respective agency)	Public Service Leadership Programme	Wide spectrum of governance work, from policy formulation to implementation	For undergraduate study in English-speaking countries: 6 years For undergraduate study in non-English speaking countries: 5 years For undergraduate study in Singapore: 4 years
Singapore Armed Forces (SAF) Scholarship	As approved by SAF	SAF	Command leadership appointments and staff appointments as force planners, military strategists or defence diplomats	
Singapore Police Force (SPF) Scholarship	As approved by SPF	Public Service Leadership Programme (Home Uniform Service)	Involved in shaping policies to address issues on public law and order and play an integral role in protecting Singapore	
PSC Scholarship (Engineering)	Various Engineering courses	Public Service Leadership Programme (PSLP) (General Phase – Engineering)	Assigned a parent agency in one of the following three engineering clusters, namely the (i) Defence and Security, (ii) Information and Communications Technology & Smart Systems and (iii) Infrastructure & Environment	
PSC Scholarship (Foreign Service)	As approved by the Ministry of Foreign Affairs (in specific countries)	Public Service Leadership Programme	Take up role of a Foreign Service Officer (FSO) (Political and Economic), posted in various countries	

PSC Scholarship (Legal Service)	International Law, International Law and Global Security, Law, Law and Diplomacy	Singapore Legal Service	Participate in the administration of justice and to advance the rule of law in Singapore	
PSC Scholarship (Teaching Service)	As approved by the respective agency	Public Service Leadership Programme	Involved in policy formulation and leadership roles in the larger Civil Service, including education	
PSC Scholarship (Public Finance)	Accountancy	Public Service Leadership Programme – Accountant-General's Department (AGD) and Auditor-General's Office (AGO)	Deepen expertise in jobs at their parent agency (either AGD or AGO). Opportunity to be posted to other agencies to gain broader perspectives on the other functions of public finance.	
PSC Scholarship (Medicine) and PSC Scholarship (Dentistry)	Dentistry and Medicine (Singapore only)	Ministry of Health	Medical Practitioners	6 years

The President's Scholarship is widely regarded as Singapore's most prestigious undergraduate scholarship. The scholarship is awarded to students who have distinguished themselves beyond excellence in academic pursuits and co-curricular activities. In awarding President's Scholarships, the PSC looks for outstanding young men and women of sound character who exemplify the ethos of the Public Service and dedication to improving the lives of Singaporeans. Since 1962, about 60 scholarships administered by the PSC are granted annually to ensure talents in the succession pipeline. The PSC scholarships are targeted at recruitment for critical high-level public service functions (Neo & Chen, 2007). Previously if these returning scholars passed a rigorous and selective interview, they were directly recruited to the administrative service (we will discuss this scheme further in the next section). Subsequently, the returnees had to be deployed throughout the service through a 4-year Management Associate Programme (MAP) before they are considered for the administrative service (Poocharoen & Lee, 2013; Davies, 2014; Lee & Rezaei, 2019). With the introduction of the Public Sector Leadership Programme (PSLP) in 2017, recipients are mostly (except under the uniform or medical track) emplaced on the Public Service Leadership Programme upon return and groomed as leaders in generalist or specialist tracks, with an outsize influence on policymaking, and therefore the lives of Singaporeans more generally.

Besides the PSC scholarships, respective agencies also offer scholarships based on their criteria and organisational needs. Recipients will also be bonded to the agencies for about 2–5 years upon their return. For example, in line with the nation's Smart Nation vision, the Smart Nation Scholarship was launched in 2018 to attract and groom a pool of deep technological talent and leaders to co-create Singapore's digital future and develop technology for the public good. Technology is not only critical to enhance productivity but as we have witnessed during the COVID-19 pandemic, from tracing, working home, home-based learning to offering government services on digital platforms, Singapore had been quick in responding to all the necessary digitisation needs. It was not only because of its matured digital infrastructure but it is also due to the ready pool of expertise who were capable to develop apps and platforms within a short period of time. Returnees from the Smart Nation Scholarship will undergo rigorous technical training under the respective talent programmes oversee by the Government Technology Agency (GovTech), the Cyber Security Agency of Singapore (CSA) and the Infocommunications Media Development Authority (IMDA) respective talent programmes and take on key roles in national Smart Nation projects. To meet the rising social needs and to encourage the new generation to pursue a career in social service, the Social Service Scholarship was also offered to individuals to undertake studies in related areas. Upon graduation, the recipients can choose to take on diverse roles in over 450 agencies across Singapore in five main social service areas namely: disability and special needs; children and youths; mental health; seniors; and families.

Recruitment

Besides attracting pre-service talents through scholarship schemes, there are also open recruitments through a central online job portal (www.careers. gov.sg) to attract fresh graduates and mid-career switchers to join the sector in various disciplines, qualifications and experience. PSD is the main institution that will work with all employers in the public sector to attract, develop, retain and engage these non-scholar officers. The officer's beginning grade when he/she first joins will be determined by his/her work experience, skills, education and personal attributes. After that, through exposure and rotations, the officer will progress based on performance, personal attributes and ability. There will be opportunities for the officer to attend training as each officer will be allocated 100 training hours per year (McNulty & Kaveri, 2019). Throughout their career in the service, officers will be exposed and get to experience a variety of jobs, different challenges and perspectives through job rotations within their agencies or across different agencies. In addition, officers can also enrol in a formal postgraduate degree at certain points of their career and support in the form of unrecorded leave or sponsorship of course fees.

Specialised pathways for executives

Specialised pathways

Most of the officers will undergo similar career progression pathways in the service with exposures to different job scopes, domains and projects to be developed throughout their career. There are also some positions that have fixed specialised career pathways. For example, the Inland Revenue Authority of Singapore (IRAS) offers one pathway for tax specialists and another pathway for managers while the Ministry of Education also offers different pathways for teachers, allied educators and executives.

Management Associates Programme (statutory boards)

As part of a decentralised public sector whereby statutory boards have the autonomy to establish their talent schemes, the statutory boards have their respective-structured MAPs designed according to their agency needs and requirements to attract fresh graduates and mid-career switchers. The

MAPs are designed as a 12-month programme, unlike the 4 years' PSLP. Over the span of 12 months, officers will be rotated among departments and functions within the same agency and will be offered the opportunity to undertake short-term overseas attachment. For example, the MAP in Enterprise Singapore is opened to fresh/recent graduates with less than 2 years of working experience. During the 12 months, officers will undergo three job rotations across different business functions to develop skills and business acumen in different fields, broadening their perspectives of the industrial and entrepreneurial landscape in Singapore (Enterprise Singapore, 2021). They will also have the opportunity to acquire global work experiences through an overseas attachment. The Singapore Tourism Board MAP is also opened to fresh graduates and also allows successful candidates to gain exposure and build knowledge in various aspects of the tourism sector through a structured training and development programme that includes a compulsory onboarding programme, an attachment to the Singapore Visitors Centre and two 21-week divisional deployments within the agency (STB, 2021). Upon completion of the 12-month MAP, the officer will be permanently deployed in the two agencies.

Leadership development schemes for senior management

There are two distinctive career development schemes for the scholarship returnees to be groomed and developed through their career in the public sector. They are namely the Public Sector Leadership Programme (PSLP) and Administrative Service (AS).

Public Sector Leadership Programme (PSLP)

PSLP replaced the Management Associates Programme (MAP) and most of the returning scholars are placed under this scheme to be developed and rewarded more systematically and competitively so that they can lead their peers in the same field and profession with credibility. Previously returning scholars are groomed as generalists and the outstanding ones will be invited to join the Administrative Service after they complete the 4-year MAP and pass the interview. Recognising the need to develop a broader base of leaders beyond the Administrative Service and responding to the need for grooming leaders who have deep expertise in key domains such as education, health care, urban planning, communications or foreign policy, the PSLP was set up in 2015, administered by PSD to create multiple job structures and career pathways, so that officers can rise up in professional roles and reach apex positions in their own fields, and not just go through the Administrative Service route (Speech by Prime Minister Lee Hsien Loong at the 2020 Annual Public Service Leadership Dinner, 17 January 2020). The apex positions include the Director of Medical Services, or the Director-General of Education, or the Chief Planner, the Accountant-General, or Chief of Government Communications. These officers can then partner and complement the AOs, as part of the larger collective public sector leadership to make up for a more balanced and resilient system.

There are two phases of the PSLP namely the general phase and the sectoral phase. The general phase is created for those with little or no work experience and they will be posted to two agencies across two sectors, for a minimum of 2 years each to develop them in core public governance capabilities. The rotations will also allow them the opportunity to explore and gain experience in at least two different sectors of the Public Service. Under the general phase, there is a structured leadership development opportunity that includes rotations, attachments, milestone programmes, inter-agency projects, and coaching and mentoring. Upon completion of the general phase, the officers may be considered for the Sectoral Phase to gain deep domain expertise and knowledge in a chosen sector; or for the AS to remain as a generalist. There are six sectors under the sectoral phase that officers may choose from, namely central administration, economy building, infrastructure and environment, security, and social, and information & communications technology and smart systems. Officers are given the developmental opportunities and critical experiences to build deep competencies in a specific sector through rotations to different agencies in a chosen sector as well as provided with training programmes to expose officers to key developments and cross-cutting issues within the sector to be developed as a specialist leader. Besides scholars, the PSLP is also opened for applications from fresh graduates and mid-career switchers. For candidates with less than 4 years of experience, they will apply for the general phase while mid-career switchers with several years of experience would need to secure a job with a public agency first before applying for the sectoral phase. In-service officers will also be considered for the PSLP via the annual 'In-Service Nomination Exercise' as nominated by their reporting officers through assessment of their performance and potential. Hence, this programme also replaces the former high-potential (HiPo) programme.

Senior management track

The Administrative Service (AS) scheme marks the cream of the crop of Singapore's civil servants – currently, there are only about 200–300 in the scheme (McNulty and Kaveri, 2019). The majority of Administrative Officers (AO) are scholars centrally appointed by PSC and their deployment designations, career paths and postings in the different sectors of the Public Service as well as to private sector companies, statutory boards and government-linked companies, are managed by the PSD. AOs could also work in other non-Civil Service organisations such as international organisations, and non-profit organisations, or even abroad. Subject to performance, they may also be appointed as directors on the boards of government-linked companies and statutory boards (PSC, 2019). As the AOs are responsible for developing and implementing national policies in consultation with the political leadership, there have been criticisms that they do not have sufficient knowledge on the ground. Therefore, AOs are invited to participate in the Community Attachment Programme (CAP) as part of their milestone training programmes to allow them to appreciate the issues on the ground and needs of the citizens, as well as the role of the grassroots organisations in engaging the residents on their well-being and concerns. AOs will also be required to attend milestone training programmes at the Civil Service College, the main training institute of the public sector at key stages of their career to equip them with skills and knowledge on policy implementation so that they can take on higher-level appointments. In addition, through the training, they will also be able to network with their peers from other agencies and with key public sector leaders. In addition to local training, they are also sent for study visits abroad to gain exposure and understanding of the political, economic and social developments in the region and the world and learn from leaders from other countries.

AOs will also be involved in inter-Agency Project Teams to collaborate with and learn from senior leaders and peers across the Public Service through inter-agency project teams such as in the whole of government collaborations like the Singapore Youth Olympic Games and Climate Change Network (Lee, 2017) to study cross-agency challenges and issues. Each AO will be mentored by a more experienced officer who will guide their personal and professional development in the Administrative Service. They will also be supported by expert coaching to facilitate their professional development. Directors of the departments in Singapore are relatively young in their mid-30s when compared to Malaysia and Thailand. The top-performing AOs will take up permanent secretary positions in the end. By their mid-30s, if the AOs' estimated potential is less than deputy secretary of the ministry, he/she would usually be asked to leave the service (Neo & Chen, 2007). A clear benefit of the Administrative Service is that Administrative Officers' remuneration sits in a different, higher pay scale, and is not tied to any particular ministry, hence facilitating a tight network of high-calibre talented officers enabling effective inter-ministry and inter-agency coordination (McNulty & Kaveri, 2019). The Administrative Officers are groomed throughout their careers to have a sound grasp of the complexities of government. Previously only returning scholars who had completed the 4-year MAP and assessment to be considered and appointed as AOs. The AS is open for application to candidates (in-service and mid-career switchers) with outstanding career history, relevant working experience and a proven track record of leadership qualities.

Performance management

Singapore is one of the earliest adopters of market-rated pay and performance-related rewards in the public sector being a strong supporter of NPM practices and has chosen to reward its talents highly based on both competency and performance. It has and continues to fine-tune the remuneration scale to stay competitive with the private sector. Its philosophy of attracting the 'best and brightest' into the service aligns with its fundamental idea to 'pay civil servants market rates for their abilities and responsibilities', to 'offer whatever salaries are necessary to attract and retain talent that it needs' (speech to parliament from Lee Hsien Loong, Minister for Trade and Industry, 17 March 1989). Based on this, a hefty increase for senior civil servants was recommended as the low salaries and slow promotion in the AS had led to high turnover. A White Paper on 'Competitive Salaries for Competent and Honest Government' was presented to Parliament on 21 October 1994 to justify the pegging of the salaries of ministers and senior civil servants to the average salaries of the top four earners in the six private sector professions of accounting, banking, engineering, law, local manufacturing companies and MNCs. Today, Singapore's ministers are the highest paid in the world and the remuneration for all officers has also shifted to fully cash-based, removing all non-cash benefits. Bonuses that correspond to the economic growth of the country are also paid to the ministers and senior-level officers.

Moving away from the seniority-based system, it has also implemented performance bonuses for all officers since the year 2000. Salary components such as merit increments and performance bonuses are tied to an officer's assessed performance. Officers who are assessed to have performed better than their peers will receive higher merit increments and performance bonuses. This ensures that officers' salaries commensurate with their contributions and abilities (PSD, 2019). Singapore's performance appraisal system runs on a quota-based bell curve. Top performers make up about 15 per cent of the distribution curve, 80 per cent will be rated as developing contributors or average, and the rest of the 5 per cent will be the poor performers (Poocharoen & Lee, 2013). There are two components: the reporting system and the ranking system. The main assessment criteria for the reporting system are personal performance targets and trait-based criteria or competencies. The ranking system also has two components: performance ranking and potential ranking. The potential ranking component affects more on the officer's promotion and is largely determined by an individual's currently estimated potential (CEP) score, which is based on competencies such as educational merits, intellectual, and leadership qualities.

The CEP system has always been a bone of contention as it seems to determine the 'fate' of an officer upon entry into the service and so it was reviewed in 2019 during the review of Civil Service's HR systems and policies to support the public sector transformation. Although it was concluded that CEP is still an important tool to assess officers' leadership potential, it will no longer be the 'single most important determinant' of his or her career development and progression and every officer should also have a rolling 5-year development roadmap that is shared with their supervisors (Chan, 2020). The move to place emphasis on helping officers to identify their potential and career goals in the short to medium term is welcomed by the public sector; however, as it is not being rolled out yet, we have not seen its implementation and effect. Nevertheless, this is a move towards a more inclusive approach to talent management and leadership development in the Singapore public sector.

4 Talent management and leadership development in Malaysia

Development and strengthening of public service managers towards achieving developmental goals

The government of Malaysia is emphasising on development of talent in the public sector, as it is the most significant resource for the public service. As the public sector is responsible for designing and implementing policies (Taylor & Wright, 2004), decisions that are carried out will have an impact on the entire people and the credibility of the government itself. Therefore, it is vital to develop key potential talented public servants with the relevant key competencies to ensure efficient public service delivery. Civil servants play an important role in the transformation and modernisation of the country and good leaders are needed at all levels of government.

Although the government has invested in various programmes and initiatives to develop key personnel within the public sector, it is still short of talented people, struggling to develop talent, and preventing talented skilful people from leaving. In addition, the education system is not producing individuals with the right skills for the position or task, resulting in talent mismatch. As one of the key aspirations of Malaysia is to enrich public service in Malaysia as a citizen centre that is having talented human capital, there is a need to strengthen the talent management of public sector managers in Malaysia. Unfortunately, leadership in the country is often seen as a kind of control mechanism as its social capital is unevenly distributed, creating vast cultural and political inequalities (Beh & Kennan, 2013) especially its constitution provides explicitly for preferential policies for Malays and indigenous groups collectively known as the Bumiputera or 'sons of the soil' leading to isolation and resentment (Lee, 2017). The Bumiputera quota system was also applied in education, employment and ownership policies in the country. The policy is further reinforced by the Malay dominance of the executive branch of government.

As part of the process to revamp its public administration for the 21st century, the Malaysian government has identified flaws within its talent management system that have impeded the progress of the bureaucracy. Some of these weaknesses include, inter alia, the ineptitude to draw the right talent due to low innovation, a mismatch of talents between the demand and supply of skills and a paucity in the number of potential employees that have the right proficiencies and useful skills. With these shortcomings in mind, the government has developed two national transformation frameworks to improve its human resource issues. Firstly, the 10th Malaysia Plan (2011–2015) was levelled at boosting human capital in the public sector through initiatives such as launching performance assessment criteria, employing and retaining skilled talent, and revolutionising the existing bureaucratic hierarchy. In addition, the 11th Malaysia Plan (2016–2020) aimed to strengthen talent management for the future of the public service through various measures, namely, recruiting specialised competent and skilful individuals on a contractual basis, employing a bottom-up approach where agencies strategise and carve out their own human resource policies according to their needs and preferences, and streamlining the curriculum for courses and training programmes in order to cultivate the appropriate leadership proficiencies in public servants (Ananthan et al., 2019).

Malaysia civil service

Malaysia is known to have the highest number of civil servants in the Southeast Asia region, recording a ratio of civil servants per population as 1:19.37 (Malaysian Digest, 2017). In Malaysia, there are 1.6 million civil servants in 240 schemes of service, out of which 28 of them fall under the purview of the public services department (Dalayga, 2020). It includes the federal public service, state public services, joint public services, education service, judiciary, legal service, police and armed forces who offer services at every level of the government, from local authorities right up to policymakers at the central agencies.

The agencies which are responsible for overseeing the public service and talent management practices in Malaysia include Jabatan Perkhidmatan Awam (JPA) or known as the Public Service Department; Suruhanjaya Perkhidmatan Awam (SPA) or the Public Services Commission; and the National Institute of Public Administration (INTAN). JPA is accountable for managing human resources in public agencies through systematic and structured human resource planning; designing relevant service schemes, organisational structures and remuneration packages to meet needs; and developing and implementing human resource policies (JPA, 2021). SPA oversees the rules and regulation on managing public servants from appointment until retirement and its functions include appointment, confirmation into service, entry in pensionable position, oversee promotion and posting, and carrying out disciplinary actions towards errant behaviours. INTAN is the training and development arm of JPA and it is committed to training officers. INTAN is equipped with a wide range of subject matter experts who train civil servants to attain a high level of competence. There is one central regional campus in Kuala Lumpur and two campuses in Kuching, Sarawak and Sabah.

Pre-service scholarship

Every year, the Government offers thousands of scholarships to excellent Malaysian students through the JPA to pursue their studies at either local or foreign higher educational institutions at Diploma and Bachelor's degree levels. Previously, the JPA overseas scholarship was only for undergraduate studies and was career-specific as the scholarship is tied to the specific preferred field of study, especially in Medicine. It is also student-specific, merit-based and need-based. At the end of the course, the scholar is bonded to serve the government for a period ranging from 6 to 10 years. Currently, the scholarship is also offered for diploma studies and encompasses a diverse range of fields. The various JPA sponsorship programmes are JPA Local Sponsorship for Diploma and Bachelor's Degree Programmes. Under the local programme, JPA offers scholarships to students who have successfully obtained admission to three types of higher educational institutions for Diploma and Bachelor's degree programmes (Table 4.1)

The JPA overseas scholarship is one of the most sought-after government scholarships in Malaysia for students to pursue tertiary education abroad. Successful recipients will undergo a pre-university programme or prepare for pre-university examinations such as A-levels at a local college. Upon completion, he or she will then apply individually to a university, taken from a list of universities in the country agreed upon in the scholarship agreement. High concentrations of scholarships are offered for disciplines deemed critical such as medicine and pharmacy (Mukherjee et al., 2017). Coupled with strong academic achievement, family's socioeconomic status and ethnicity are major criteria. Further outlined in the Revised Budget 2016 and to ensure that the country gets the optimum returns and benefits from substantial investments earmarked for the sponsorship programme, the government has introduced a new model of JPA sponsorship schemes that fund the scholarship with a loan repayable upon graduation. Repayment of the Loan is divided into two schemes, which are Ordinary Loan (OL) and Convertible Loan (CL). For the OL scheme, the borrower is required to reimburse the full amount of loan received during their study, upon completion of their study. Whereas for the CL scheme, a discount can be granted for as much as 75 per cent (off the full amount of the loan

Table 4.1 Overview of scholarships offered by JPA (PSD)

Sponsorship Type	Courses	Eligibility	Financial Support
Sponsorship for Diploma Courses at Polytechnics	Various Diploma programmes offered by Polytechnics, Ministry of Education	• Must be a Malaysian citizen • Open to all students possessing Sijil Pelajaran Malaysia (SPM) only • Not older than 19 years • Already registered for year 1 of the programme at the polytechnic • Possess at least Grade 6C in Bahasa Malaysia and at least 4B in 6 subjects	Scholarship
Sponsorship for Diploma & Bachelor's Degree Courses at Universities	Critical courses such as Medicine, Dentistry and Pharmacy; Pure Sciences; Applied Sciences; Professional Arts; Arts; Technology; and Islamic Studies	• Must be a Malaysian citizen • Opened to year 1 students who have been accepted by the abovementioned universities. • Not older than 19 years for Diploma programmes • Not older than 24 years for Bachelor's degree programmes • SPM results – Grade 2A for at least 7 subjects • STPM results – at least Principal B in 4 subjects • Diploma – minimum 3.30 CGPA score • STAM results – at least 4 Mumtaz and 5 Jayyid Jiddah (Islamic studies) • Passed the matriculation examination by the Ministry of Education/University's Foundation Studies and score at least 3.30 CGPA	• Scholarships are being awarded to excellent local students in fields such as Medicine, Dentistry, Pharmacy, Engineering and Science and Technology • Loans are being given only to students in local polytechnics. • Loans also being provided to sponsor overseas undergraduate students to support their tuition fees who face financial problems.
Sponsorship for Overseas Bachelor's Degree Programmes at Overseas	Various Bachelor courses at prestigious overseas universities	• Must be below 18 years old • Undergo locally conducted preparatory courses for about 1–2 years and pass the preparatory course with distinctions • Offered a place in any of the top universities in the USA, Britain or Australia listed by JPA	Scholarship

received), if they did fulfil the criteria, i.e., pursuing first-degree education; achieving at least 2nd Class Lower Division or a CGPA above of 2.75 or equivalent; and succeed in completing the study within the period prescribed, without any extension.

Upon completion of the course, the scholar is bonded to serve the government for a period ranging from 6 to 10 years. The Talent Acceleration in Public Service (TAPS) programme led by the JPA with the Razak School of Government (RSOG) and TalentCorp aims to channel and prepare the best and brightest from among the JPA scholars into the public service. However, job availability in the government is not guaranteed; therefore, if the scholar is not able to secure a job within a year upon return, he or she is allowed to apply for employment in the private sector. JPA has also initiated the Scholarship Talent Attraction and Retention (STAR) programme, which is a joint initiative between JPA and TalentCorp. STAR enables scholars who are interested in working in the private sector to service their bonds by working in leading companies (mostly government-linked companies), pre-identified by the government as in the key sectors to drive the economic growth.

Recruitment and training

Full-time employment

The Malaysian public sector also has open recruitment for various vacancies as and when they are available. Recruitment of new officers is by SPA and done fully through a computerised system, known as the Continuous Recruitment System or eSMSM in short. This system was first introduced in January 1997. The employment of eSMSM allows job applications from Malaysian citizens to be made at any time throughout the year online via the official PSC portal at www.spa.gov.my. SPA has also upgraded the job application system from the previous SPA8i system to the new Employment Registration System (SPA9). SPA9 has a job-matching feature that would offer applicants the most suitable posts based on the requirements and educational backgrounds and additionally, make it easier and faster for candidates to apply for and be offered employment.

There are 28 schemes of services under the purview of the JPA and they are divided into three service groups, namely Top Management Group, Management and Professional Group and Support Group under the provisions of the New Remuneration System (SSB) and subsequently the Malaysia Remuneration System (SSM). The Top Management Group embodies strategic posts intended as the promotional grade from the qualified Management and Professional Group consisting of Premier Grade C and above.

The Management and Professional Group is a scheme of services with a minimum entry qualification of bachelor's degree or other higher qualification as recognised by the Government. The Support Group is a scheme of services with an entry qualification of diploma level or other equivalent qualification recognised by the Government (JPA, 2021).

Shortlisted candidates will be invited for interviews and required to sit for examinations before they are appointed. Salaries, scheme of service, fixed remuneration of public service, housing allowance and subsistence allowance will commensurate with their qualifications. Attempts were also made to balance out its ethnic proportions through the direct recruitment of non-Malay civil servants. This was accomplished through a private–public collaboration between the PSC and nongovernmental organisations (NGOs) such as the Federation of Chinese Association Malaysia to recruit Chinese civil servants (Woo, 2015). Officers will also have opportunities for training and development in the course of their careers.

'MyStep' (short-term employment programme)

The Malaysian government introduced a new initiative called 'MyStep' (Short-Term Employment Programme) where 50,000 contract jobs are expected to be offered in the public sector, government bodies and agencies, and in Government-Linked Corporations (GLCs) to provide work for Malaysians (Renushara, 2020). This initiative starts in January 2021. The government has allocated RM700 million for this initiative and the GLCs are expected to provide 15,000 job opportunities to fresh grads via apprenticeship programmes mainly in the technical and financial fields. The rest of the 35,000 job opportunities comprise nurses, community welfare officers and substitute teachers.

As part of the apprenticeship programme, graduates will receive a stipend of RM1,000 monthly for up to 3 months, within the stipulated apprenticeship period. Employers will receive an RM4,000 grant for providing training programmes for the apprentices.

Senior management development

Administrative and diplomatic scheme

The Administrative and Diplomatic scheme, or better known in Malay as the Pegawai Tadbir dan Diplomatik (PTD) scheme is the earliest 'premier' public service track, going back to 1904. Like Singapore, PTD officers are the key policymakers in the Malaysian civil service. Many top government posts, in Malaysia and abroad, are held by PTD officers. There are currently about 9,000–10,000 PTD officers engaged in diverse levels of employment in the Administrative and Diplomatic Service and hold strategic and key leadership roles, many of them are in Putrajaya (Chin, 2011). Most of the senior civil servants are ADS officers who are generalists and they are considered the pillar and cream of the civil service of which they are involved in all stages of policy formulation and its implementation. They also have opportunities to be transferred to different organisations as well as seconded to private organisations.

Application to the scheme is open to all outside the service and in-service officers. The minimum entry requirement is a bachelor's degree with honour (from any discipline) from an institution that is recognised by the government. However, being a premier service, the selection process for the ADS is more rigorous in comparison to other services from the Managerial and Professional Group. Short-listed candidates first sit a written test that covers topics on general knowledge about Malaysia and its environment, problem-solving skills, comprehension, and written essays in English and Malay language. Those who fare well in the examinations will be short-listed to attend the PTD Assessment Center (PAC). The PAC is a 3-day programme and is held in all INTAN campuses throughout the country. The candidates will be assessed on the basis of various competencies based on personal qualities (including leadership potential and teamwork), knowledge and skills. Aspects of knowledge that are assessed include the ability to generate ideas that are mature in outlook, substantive and relevant. Skills that are assessed in the PAC are public-speaking skills, communication skills and parliamentary debating skills. Apart from the three competency areas, candidates are also evaluated on their physical endurance. Marks obtained by the candidates throughout the PAC are then ranked and submitted to the PSC, where only the best will be called for an interview. Only those who successfully went through the interview will be appointed as an ADS officer. The National Institute of Public Administration (INTAN) is responsible for developing and conducting assessments for all candidates.

Upon appointment as a PTD officer, the officer will need to go through four more stages of training, the first being a 10-day foundation course called 'PTD Unggul'. That inducts ADS officers on the excellent work culture and the role they have to play in fulfilling the aspirations of the nation and its stakeholders. At the end of the course, the young recruits are informed of their job assignments and which ministries or departments they are attached to, either at the state or federal level. After that, the officer will undergo a 6-month on-the-job training, followed by another compulsory 6-month Diploma in Public Administration (DPA) course at INTAN's main campus in Bukit Kiara to be equipped with knowledge and skills pertaining to values and ethics which are significant in developing civil servants with integrity, accountability and skill before they are officially appointed as PTD officers (Manaf, 2010).

At present, it is noted that most PTD officers enter the service with limited work experience. Therefore, there have been suggestions about improving the recruitment process, to allow applicants to at least have 3 years of experience in any branch of the government and need to have a global mindset and good negotiation skills. There should also be a recurrent assessment of the officers' performance to determine if they should still be in the scheme or be asked to leave the scheme. However, so far, there have not been any further developments to the scheme.

Fast-track scheme

High-performing in-service officers who have the capacity to assume higher leadership roles are identified on the basis of the annual performance appraisal process. Identified officers are given more challenging projects, assignments or sent for prime postings. They can also be offered study sponsorships for higher education at the master's or doctoral levels. However, there is no explicit roadmap for this group of officers and they are not guaranteed higher positions upon completion of their studies or assignments. The fast-track system was introduced in 2016 and aims to identify high-potential public servants to be placed in leadership positions. Moving away from the seniority-based promotion practice, under the fast-track system, the Promotions Board can promote any individual over a senior officer if he or she demonstrates the potential to lead. To qualify, candidates must score at least 90 per cent in their annual appraisals for three consecutive years; score a Band 5 in the Middle Management Leadership Assessment Programme or the Advanced Leadership Development and Assessment Programme. The candidate would also be required to undergo psychometric and physical fitness tests. In addition, candidates in the Professional and Management group must score at least a Band 4 in their English Language Proficiency Assessment (ELPA) test conducted by INTAN.

Performance-based pay increment

Flexible income increment

The public service in Malaysia has moved away from the seniority-based system and is currently operating on a performance-based system that applies throughout the service. The fixed-pay increment structure is determined by officers' performance. Although there is no performance-based bonus payout, promotion is determined by the officer's performance. The

New Remuneration Scheme (NRS) came into effect in 1992 to enhance the objectivity and reliability of civil servants' pay and career advancements by linking their performance with the rewards system. It was also intended to boost the capability of the bureaucracy in securing and keeping inventive, resourceful and gifted personnel and instil a working ethos based on excellence and efficiency (Siddiquee, 2006).

The NRS superseded the previously utilised linear salary model for a matrix salary schedule to allow a larger extent of flexibility in income progression. Based on a public servant's performance, his recompense can advance in one of four distinctive tracks: static, horizontal, vertical and diagonal. The maximum pay increment is 3 per cent of the vertical salary movement and 2 per cent for diagonal progression (Manaf, 2010; Beh, 2016). For instance, an excellent performer will move diagonally along this improved pay structure to enjoy double annual increments. To assist in the implementation of the NRS, a new performance evaluation scheme was also enacted to curtail bias and be more transparent in its approach to appraise an employee's performance. This new performance evaluation procedure was accomplished by decentralising the process whereby a panel is set up to study and deliberate on diverse aspects such as an employee's performance and the type of his salary progression. However, these reforms proposed through the NRS and the improved performance evaluation procedure generated dissatisfaction among some civil servants because there was no clarity. Another competency-based pay system, known as the Malaysian Remuneration System (SSM), was introduced in 2002 to deal with the problems in the NRS (Putra and Hizatul, 2004). While the SSM did not completely replace the NRS, it provided an alternative method of choice for performance evaluation for civil servants (Siddiquee, 2006).

In 2012, the New Civil Service Remuneration Scheme (SBPA) was planned to be implemented, which will enforce a new exit policy for civil servants who do not perform or wish to transfer to other agencies or the private sector. However, it was withdrawn shortly after the announcement after it had come under criticism from the lower-ranking civil servants as the scheme was found to benefit the top officials. It reverted to an improved SSM whereby the annual salary increment structure would be revised from the matrix-salary schedule to the minimum-maximum-salary schedule, with a yearly increment of between RM80 and RM320 (7–13 per cent) for Grades 1 to 54, depending on their grades (Sivanandam, 2012).

Bonuses/special assistance for civil servants for selected Malaysian states

Some Malaysian state governments such as Perak, Sarawak and Penang are offering bonuses or extra financial assistance for their civil servants. For instance, the Perak government is handing out 1 month's salary as special financial assistance for civil servants to be paid by the end of December 2020 in recognition for their rendered service and dedication in discharging their duties. In Sarawak, state civil service personnel will receive a bonus adding up to one and a half months of their basic salary, or a minimum amount of RM2,000, to be made before the end of the year, in recognition of the public servants' support and contribution to the state. Additionally, according to the chief minister, members of the federal civil service who are serving in the state will receive a one-off payment of RM500 to be made in the first quarter of 2021. Likewise, the Penang state government proffered special financial assistance for about 4,000 civil servants amounting to a half-month salary or a minimum amount of RM1,000 to be paid by December 2020. This bonus is made to civil servants in appreciation for their services in planning and discharging policies and development plans for the state.

5 Talent management and leadership development in Thailand

Development of ICT talents in a lean and decentralised bureaucracy

Against the backdrop of political instability and violence since 1992, major reforms in the Thailand public sector had taken place at both national and sector system levels. Most notable was the decentralisation of power from the national government to localities, the creation of new forms of public organisation, and the systemwide reform of the public administration system (Kelly et al., 2012). All these major reforms were initiated by public officers with support from politicians and parliament. Over the past 20 years, the administrative system in Thailand has undergone several changes. Thailand has a unique political environment context influencing the changing faces of bureaucracy, unlike its neighbouring countries which were under colonial rule (Dana, 2014). New initiatives were introduced in the public sector to control the size or number of public agencies as well as the shape and cost of public personnel, oversight by the Civil Service Development Commission. These include: firstly, in the setting up of a new agency, it must not duplicate any similar work that has been carried out by any existing agency. Secondly, the new agency must be a provincial office and not a central one. Lastly, staff from other existing agencies or units should be given priority to fill the vacancies in the new agency. However, due to the expansion for economic development, healthcare services, education and local administration, instead of reducing the number of staff, it resulted in an increase of approximately 53,000 civil servants over 10 years from 1980 to 1990 (Tamronglak, 2020).

Since the 1990s, digital government strategies have been among the key policy initiatives for Southeast Asia to strengthen economic development and addressing societal problems. The Thai government particularly has been leading ICT-enabled transformation of government and many initiatives have been developed, including the recent notion of 'e-Government 4.0'. A key feature of these efforts is strong centralised political support, and announcement of, Thailand's Digital Government Plan 2017–2022. Thailand's current digital government strategy is tightly connected to the country's economic and social development plans, specifically the overarching 'Thailand 4.0' strategy which targets the middle-income trap, unbalanced economic growth and inequality. Central agencies, i.e., the Ministry of Digital Economy and Society and the Electronic Government Agency will have a significant role in leading such government-wide, executive-driven reform and coordinating digital transformation (Sagarika et al., 2018). These central agencies provide policymaking and direct central resources towards the different levels of government institutions and to pursue consistent digital government policies across levels and across sectors via stronger instruments of central control. However, the severe lack of ICT experience and digital capacity (e.g., 'digital literacy') among Thai public servants has been a growing concern. Recruitment of new Thai public servants via a Civil Service Exam also does not prioritise ICT proficiency, and upon employment, exposure to ICT in everyday work is still often limited. To address these gaps, new training programmes have been developed to increase the digital literacy of public servants.

Thailand public sector

The Thailand public sector consists of about 2.19 million personnel, working in 20 ministries and 166 departments. This is excluding the Ministry of Defence. Of these, 81.89 per cent of the civil servants work in the central and provincial administration and about one-third are ordinary civil servants under the jurisdiction of the Office of the Civil Service Commission (OCSC). (Yavaprabhas, 2018). This is equivalent to 3.15 per cent of the country's Civil Service population and 5.45 per cent of its workforce (OCSC, 2021). With the enactment of the 2008 Civil Service Act, there were namely four types of positions in the civil service, namely: executive, managerial, knowledge worker and general positions under the new classification system (Huque & Jongruck, 2020). Public administration in Thailand comprises three levels namely: national or central administration, provincial administration and local administration. At present, there are 20 ministries and 161 departments at the national level. At the provincial level, there are 77 provinces. Within each province, the next tier is amphoe (district) and under amphoe is tambon (subdistrict). Currently, there are 878 amphoes and 7,255 tambon (as of March 2016) (Yavaprabhas, 2018).

The OCSC is the main agency that oversees the talent scheme and development of the ordinary civil servants working in the central administration. The OCSC is a government agency with the Secretary-General as the head and reports directly to the Prime Minister. The OCSC serves as the secretariat of the Civil Service Commission (CSC) and the central human resources management agency of the civil service. Its functions are also to support government agencies on the management of human resources and to protect the merit system in the civil service that enables officials, under the appropriate quality of work life, to perform their duties professionally conforming to merit and ethical standards and good governance principle in order to ensure public benefits and national sustainable development (OCSC, 2021). Another agency is the Office of the Public Sector Development Commission (OPDC) which is responsible for giving recommendations and suggestions to the minister cabinet on the structure of bureaucracy, budgeting system, personnel system, moral virtue and ethics standard, compensation and other public sector practices. The Civil Service Commission (CSC) of Thailand is responsible for public service human resource management and deployment through workforce planning and involvement in HR policy formulation. Prior to the Civil Service Act 1992, the composition of the Civil Service Commission from a body comprised merely of experts changed to a combination of ex officio, elected and appointed commissioners. These elected commissioners are representatives of line departments, reflecting the principle of collaboration between central and line agencies. The CSC role also became more strategic, as the Act provided for an advisory role to the Cabinet on the management aspects in the civil service, not only for ordinary civil servants but for the overall civil service as well.

The Civil Service Training Institute (CSTI) was established in 1980 to serve as the training arm of the OCSC. Its major functions are to enhance the formulation of training and development policy, to provide training leadership and to coordinate the training activities of departments and ministries. King Prajadhipok's Institute (KPI) also conducts training courses for central officers and local administrators. KPI is an independent, academic, public organisation under the supervision of Thailand's National Assembly. Besides conducting courses directly, KPI also coordinates and cooperates with local, foreign and international agencies to offer training and development opportunities to officers in the public sector.

Government scholarships

There are several types of government scholarships available to high-school students and Bachelor's degree holders. The two main ones are the King's Scholarship and Royal Thai Government Scholarship for non-specific agencies and allocated upon agencies' requirements. For the former, scholars know exactly where they are bonded to upon graduation, while for the latter the scholar chooses where they wish to serve after they return from their studies. Provided there are openings, their wish is often granted. There are cases where scholars return without a relevant agency to accommodate them, causing frustration among scholars due to the mismatch of acquired skills and agencies' needs. About 300 scholars are selected each year (Sivaraks, 2011). Contrary to the Singapore scholarship scheme, these scholars are neither put on a special track nor are they provided with different incentive structures to excel in the system but they are bonded. Scholars must serve twice the amount of time taken to study.

The OCSC also collaborated with the Ministry of Education and Ministry of Foreign Affairs to introduce the One District One Scholarship (ODOS) in 2004 to provide a chance of international education to outstanding students from poor families with the aim of broadening opportunities for local development. Recipients will be contractually obliged to work for the Thai government upon returning from abroad. To grow the science, technology, engineering and mathematics (STEM) sector, OCSC also offers two science and technology scholarships, namely, the Development of Science and Mathematics Talented Project (DPST) and Ministry of Science and Technology (MST) scholarship schemes, for top-performing students to study science and technology subjects in local and overseas universities (Sumonta et al., 2018).

Tight recruitment policy

In 2000, the government was forced to keep the public sector lean by implementing the early retirement policy for those 45 years and above as well as the cessation of recruitment of newcomers. Subsequently, in the following 10 years, the government continued to keep the bureaucracy small with very little recruitment of new officers. There are three routes a person can opt to join the civil service: firstly through a competitive examination, consisting of three testing stages – general knowledge, specific knowledge and position suitability; secondly through selection, applied where departments and the CSC deem it appropriate to apply different recruitment and selection criteria and procedures; and thirdly through special appointment, applied when departments are authorised by the CSC to recruit personnel for appointment as experts, professionals or specialists as required for the benefit of the civil service (Poocharoen & Lee, 2013; Tamronglak, 2020). For the development of the officers under OCSC purview, strategic workforce planning was applied in the public sector and the OCSC competency model composing of 17 skills was developed to evaluate the quality of the workforce to determine development needs of necessary skills, core competencies and managerial competencies so that respective officers can be sent to attend relevant training courses. In addition, a new, large-scale training programme has also been implemented for increasing the digital literacy and ICT proficiency of public servants across the country. This training embeds ICT in everyday government practice and takes a consistent 'whole-of-government' approach to deliver e-Government 4.0 across the public sector (Sagarika et al., 2018).

Although the recruitment is small, nevertheless the government launched a minimum pay reform to raise the monthly salary of civil servants to 15,000 Baht (approximately US$420) in 2013 to boost the morale of government officials and to attract fresh university graduates to join the service (TDRI, 2014).

Leadership development schemes

Public Sector Executive Development Programme (PSED)

The Public Sector Executive Development Programme (PSED) is a career scheme that aims to attract excellent young individuals to join the public sector at the mid-level entry point. The PSED is led by the OPDC, the officers are recruited and trained for 22 months and upon their graduation, they are sent to work in strategic departments and provinces. The participants go through not only intensive theory or classroom-based training on public management and leadership, but they are also trained in practice by being seconded to three groups of public-sector leaders and one private-sector leader for about 2 years. The programme offers a mentorship system exposing participants to mentors, coaches and advisers, all of whom play different roles in the training programme. The objectives of the scheme are: to develop highly effective change agents who have the abilities to be visionary thinkers, developers, planners and operators; and to deploy change agents to the strategic units and drive their strategic plans into action.

High Performance and Potential System (HiPPS)

Led by the OCSC, the HiPPS scheme has three objectives: (1) attract, maintain and motivate high-potential individuals within the civil service; (2) continuously and systematically develop them; and (3) prepare highly qualified, experienced and well-rounded leaders for senior levels. In order to develop and retain high performers who work in crucial domains in the Thai public sector, OCSC introduced the High Performance and Potential System (HiPPS). It started out as a pilot project with 8 agencies onboard in 2003. It has been implemented since 2004 and in 2006, HiPPS was extended to all civil service departments. As of 2017, there are more than 370 government officials from 100 government agencies who have participated in the scheme. This scheme was initiated on the basis of the talent management processes of selection, retention, development, motivation and delegation of talented government officials. The main purpose of the HiPPS is to help high performers to utilise their maximum potential in their assigned job and to ensure that they will act as the drivers in the government sector (OCSC, 2009b, p. 13).

The selection process of the HiPPS is sophisticated and is designed to ensure those qualified individuals are selected. Approximately only 2 per cent of government officials in each agency are appointed to join the system. In the development process, the HiPPS developed talented officials according to the workplace learning method. Job rotation, coaching and systematic training were provided. This was done under a minimum-standard time frame, monetary and non-monetary rewards, as well as an effective performance appraisal system. In addition, career path planning by an experience accumulation framework (EAF) was included to complete the system (OCSC, 2009a, pp. 14–15). It can be seen that the HiPPS is aligned. Effective human resource strategies require organisations to have the ability to, firstly, be able to attract and recruit high calibre talents into the service. Secondly, reward and recognise high performance through monetary and non-monetary incentives. Monetary incentives will be in terms of salary increment and promotion opportunities while non-monetary incentives will be opportunities for officers to undergo leadership development through workplace learning strategies such as job rotation, secondment, local and overseas training, short-term attachments, mentorship, challenging project assignments and postgraduate studies opportunities (Poocharoen & Lee, 2013; Lee & Rezaei, 2019). Thirdly, the right expectation should be created for organisations in the future to understand more effectively and respond to individual expectations at work. The challenge is to enable the key motivators of responsibility, achievement and feeling of self-worth to become common currency throughout the organisation rather than the preserve of the minority, accomplished in an environment where the manager builds productive relationships with all employees. Finally, investment in employees should be intentional by providing higher-quality training and development and improved career management.

HiPPS is not open to the public, only for in-service officers who have demonstrated high potential and high performance. The supervisors in the bureaus and agencies must identify high-performing individuals to take part in the programme and develop a clear experience accumulation framework (EAF) for the candidate. Candidates must perform outstandingly throughout to receive higher pay of about 1 per cent of his or her usual monthly income. Candidates from the Public Sector Executive Development Programme (PSED) need to pass the English exam in order to enter the programme. HiPPS constantly work with agencies to understand and identify training needs especially corresponding to a new era of globalisation, new public sector innovation and Smart Nation. Based on this, OCSC will work with external training institutions locally and overseas to design training and courses for the officers. For example, a group of 100 HiPPS officers was nominated by OCSC in 2017 to attend 1-week Competency-Based Development Program for Thailand Civil Servants in NCPA at NTU, Singapore. The participants came from various ministries in the central government. Many of them were specialists in the respective fields including medical doctors, accountants, lawyers and IT professionals. We will look into the training programme in details in chapter 9 and its relevance to capacity building and leadership development of the Thai middle and senior level officers.

New Wave Leadership Development Programme (NWLDP)

The New Wave Leadership Development Programme (NWLDP) is a 1-month training programme designed for high-calibre mid-level bureaucrats administered by OSCS. The stated objective is to promote a network of high-potential officials in various departments (Sivaraks, 2011, p. 128). Officers are sent for overseas study visits to ASEAN countries – for example, Singapore – to attend a workshop on leadership. The programme aims to build networks among civil service officers among different ASEAN countries to share knowledge and experience in areas such as e-learning, governance, leadership, organisational development and performance improvement, in responding to the globalisation trend of inclusiveness and increase collaboration among Asian countries. The programme was renamed as 'ASEAN Plus New-Wave Leadership Development' in 2017. The objectives include:

- To develop cutting-edge capacities of 'ASEAN Plus New-Wave Leaders' among participants in preparation for their future task as public officers who are ready to lead and manage effectively in both domestic and international arenas.
- To create awareness and understanding of the new outlook for policy-making, leadership and decision-making for sustainable development, especially the innovations of HR within the public service, in a fast-changing world.
- To promote harmonious relation and productive network among participants which will, in turn, enhance better collaboration between governments of ASEAN member countries and OCSC partner countries.

Performance management and competency-based assessment

The Third Civil Service Act of 1992 concentrated on the democratic, managerial and strategic elements which highlighted the importance of encouraging performance through compensation and reward mechanisms (Sivaraks, 2011). In 2006, the systems of competency, performance management and meritocracy were initiated. OCSC is responsible for the design, implementation and evaluation. HR scorecards, individual development plans and individual KPIs were developed for officers in the central administration. To ensure promotion is based on merit, the CSC delegates authority to departmental civil service subcommissions and ministerial subcommissions to decide promotions and appointments

The OPDC also created a bonus-like scheme for government officers based on the department's performance. The set of performance indicators were assigned by OPDC. With this bonus-like scheme, senior officers and department heads were eligible for as much as 12 months of basic salary (Yavaprabhas, 2018). However, the bonus scheme only benefitted mainly the senior officers, while low ranking officers who contribute to the performance only received a small part of the bonus money. At present, the bonus scheme is not as effective as at the beginning as the among of bonus allocated by the government is much smaller.

6 Talent management and leadership development in Cambodia

Strengthening of institutional and human resource capacity of middle and senior officials

The development of the nation's economy and civil service truly began during the 2000s. This is evident in the various strategies and national agendas that have been legislated to stimulate institutional improvements, economic development and good governance (World Bank Group, 2018). For instance, the initial Rectangular Strategy Phase I in 2004 by the Royal Government of Cambodia is a thorough programme to boost sustainable growth of the nation and diminish poverty through diverse strategies such as augmenting the capacity of public institutions, improving the public sector's efficacy, safeguarding the country's natural assets and producing employment opportunities for citizens. Furthermore, as part of this Strategy, the government championed the National Program for Administrative Reform (NPAR) to renovate the civil service by streamlining the bureaucracy, distributing powers to the communes and simplifying the process of public service deliveries (Sen, 2004). In a like manner, subsequent agendas embraced by the government – Rectangular Strategy Phase II (Sen, 2008), Rectangular Strategy Phase III (Sen, 2013), Rectangular Strategy Phase IV (Sen, 2018) – aim to broaden and expand on the four identified themes of growth, employment, equity and efficiency through continuously building upon past reformations to ultimately catalyse economic advancement that will put the nation in the upper middle-income category (World Bank Group, 2018).

As stated in the Rectangular Strategy, phase 3 the Royal Government of Cambodia recognises that it is crucially important to strengthen institutional and human resource capacity to assure sustainability and efficiency in the implantation of the state reform programmes in order to achieve goals of socioeconomic development and poverty reduction in Cambodia. In this sense, three mains reform programmes have been actively implemented and provided good progress to support successful socioeconomic development.

Those main reform programmes are Public Administration Reform (PAR), Public Financial Management Reform (PFM) and Decentralization and De-concentration Reform (D&D) for Subnational democratic Development. Based on the training needs analysis conducted, strengthening institutional and human resource development within the public sector are of the highest priority. It is not only on the skills development for technical and mid-level administrative officials but also for senior government officials and leaders in the areas of leadership, management, public administration, policy and governance.

Cambodia became a lower-middle-income country in 2015 and the task of delivering public services continues to become more complex (World Bank, 2020). As the country envisages to become an upper middle-income country by 2030 and a high-income economy by 2050, more Cambodians are now seeking better and efficient public services. Therefore, the Cambodian civil service will need to attract qualified, talented and hard-working people who are motivated towards a better governance outcome for Cambodia and to support the country's development vision (World Bank, 2020). As a developing low-income country, Cambodia still requires financial assistance from international organisations and institutions to develop civil service. There is also concentration on rapidly improving the quality of education in the country and also the need for competent and highly educated senior officials and leaders to lead the country to achieve its goal.

Cambodia civil service

As of 2020, there are about 220,000 civil servants across the country, including 43,849 national civil servants and 174,786 at subnational levels (Xinhua, 2020). All civil servants in Cambodia are currently employees of ministries and institutions of the Royal Government of Cambodia (RGC). Among those, a substantial portion of civil servants is appointed for positions at subnational offices of national ministries. The three largest groups of civil servants are the Ministry of Education, Ministry of Health, and Ministry of Interior, which comprise 83 per cent of total civil servants in subnational offices.

The two agencies that are responsible for the management and development of civil servants in Cambodia are the Ministry of Civil Service (MSC) and the Royal School of Administration (RSA). The MSC is the policy implementing arm of the Royal Government of Cambodia (RGC) and mandated to carry out administrative reform in the country. It has the mission of leading, managing and developing the public sector of Cambodia. Its responsibilities include developing and implementing Human Resource policies and overseeing the appointment, management, development and retirement of the civil servants. The RSA comes directly under the MSC and is responsible for the training of future administrative staff as well as to provide in-depth training and capacity building for existing civil servants. Students and interns receive training from senior officials and the school also constantly establishes institutional ties with other regional and international schools of governance and public administration to learn from best practices.

The Economics and Finance Institute (EFI), which was established in 1997 and promoted to be a General department of the Ministry of Economy and Finance (MEF) in July 2015, is also actively involved in the training and capacity development for government officials in Cambodia in the area of Public Economic and Financial Management. The courses offered by EFI were mainly conducted by in-service senior officials or in collaboration with other international training institutions or multilateral organisations under sponsorship. For example, one such cooperation was between EFI and NTU to organise and deliver a series of training programmes for senior public officials from Cambodia to learn about the experiences of Singapore with regard to public sector leadership, policy and governance. The programme was co-funded by the MEF, Cambodia and the Temasek Foundation International (TFI) of Singapore. There are plans to develop EFI into a full-fledge training institution with dedicated premises and facilities.

Government scholarships

Senior-level officers

Foreign governments around the world have made scholarships an important part of their aid to Cambodia. Since the downfall of the Khmer Rouge in 1979, Cambodia has received scholarships from various countries such as Russia, OECD countries and China. From 1980 to 2014, Cambodia sent 14,692 students abroad (MoEYS, 2015). However, these scholarships are not specifically for individuals who wish to pursue a career in the public sector. Government scholarships in Cambodia are not open to high-school leavers but successful applicants to the Grade A scheme of service (for bachelor's degree and above) who graduated from elite universities will be offered scholarships to pursue a Ph.D. These scholarships are supported either by the government or development partner – for example, UNDP, World Bank, ASEAN. Upon completion of their studies, they will be bonded for 5 years and are required to work for the government.

A joint effort in training between the Royal School of Administration of Cambodia (ERA) and the French National School of Administration (ENA) aims to support the capacity building of Cambodian civil servants.

Additionally, the French Government endeavours to train Cambodian senior civil servants through collaborating with the international body of Francophone nations (Organisation Internationale de la Francophonie (OIF)) and co-financing scholarships for these civil servants to pursue higher degrees in France (Sophanith, 2020). This assistance intends to concomitantly aid efforts by the Royal Government of Cambodia to contain COVID-19 in the country.

Teacher-candidates

To sustain Cambodia's economic development and enhance its competitiveness, scholarships are also provided to eligible teacher-candidates from disadvantaged areas to undertake a 1-year pre-service training at the National Institute of Education (NIE). As increasing the pool of upper secondary graduates is critical to improving the quality of the workforce and expanding the tertiary sector, scholarships are offered to recruit teachers to teach in rural and acute-shortage areas. This scholarship is sponsored by the Asian Development Bank (ADB) and is wholly administered and implemented by the Ministry of Education, Youth and Sport (MoEYS 2015) and the Directorate General of Education (DGE), Directorate General of Policy and Planning (DGPP), and the National Institute of Education (NIE) (ADB, 2016). The scholarships will be spread over 4 years and proportionally distributed among the science and mathematics subjects. Upon completion of the pre-service training, the trainees are assigned by the government to the schools.

Recruitment

Under the current recruitment system in Cambodia, civil servants are employed on an en bloc basis. The hiring process of public officials is decentralised in Cambodia, each ministry or agency first decides on the number of employees it wants to employ for the year and the broad types of qualifications it wants to look for in candidates, and then recruits them accordingly. But the vacancies are not made known publicly. After they are recruited, specific roles or designation of work will be allocated to them. Subsequently, new employees will receive the necessary training to equip them to effectively perform their roles (World Bank, 2020). The government will authorise the recruitment of 6,106 new civil servants in 2021 as new recruitment was suspended in 2020 due to the COVID-19 pandemic. The recruitment of the new civil servants is further broken down to 3,600 in the Ministry of Education; 1,300 in the Ministry of Health; 178 in the Ministry of Justice; 170 in the Ministry of Interior; 5 in the Ministry of National Assembly Senate Relations and Inspection; and 8 each in the Ministry of Civil Service and Ministry of Mines and Energy (Socheath, 2020).

There is also no specific career development or fast-track scheme available in the public sector. All candidates are required to take the entrance examinations for grades A, B and C. Grade A is for fresh graduates, B for candidates who attained an associate degree of vocational qualification and Grade C is for high-school leavers. The subjects of examination were Economics, Accounting, Taxation, Computer and English. It was not easy to pass the examination; out of 15,000 candidates who sat for the exam in 2011, only 300 passed and became public officials. There are also candidates who become contract staff under internship who are eligible to become full-time officials without taking the exam, subject to approval from a minister of the civil service. Mid-career entrants from the private sector are also exempted from the exams except for those applying to the Ministry of Education.

Digital training for civil servants

In a new initiative launched by the United Nations Development Program (UNDP) to connect grassroots ideas with technology and real-time data to effectively address global challenges, Cambodia's public sector will be digitally linked with other nations. Known as the UNDP Accelerator Labs schemes, this initiative focuses on public sector innovations in Cambodia and aims to transform civil servants' mindsets in order to ensure enhanced public service delivery. The Cambodian government purposes to train civil servants and public sector staff on this novel initiative.

Fast-track scheme for teachers

While it is noted that there is no known specific scheme for general civil servants, but in the move to improving the quality of education in the country, the country recognises the importance of developing teachers especially in primary and secondary schools. Many of these teachers do not have any university education and they only require 2 years of additional training after completing secondary school (i.e., 12+2 system) to be engaged as a teacher. However, the government is planning to raise the minimum requirement to 12+4, i.e., new teachers will be required to hold a bachelor's degree while existing teachers are encouraged to participate in a fast-track programme to meet the new criteria.

In line with the Upper Secondary Education Sector Development Programme sponsored by Asian Development Bank (ADB), to strengthen Science, Technology, Engineering, Mathematics (STEM) education, there are training and professional development opportunities offered to STEM teachers and administrators. Training is provided to equip them with full technical knowledge and pedagogical skills and an 18-day leadership training course designed for school principals. To improve the deployment of teachers in disadvantaged provinces and in schools with a shortage of teachers, additional hardship allowances and other teacher incentives are provided to teachers who teach in rural and remote areas. In addition, teaching housing units will also be constructed in areas of high need. This includes disadvantaged provinces, upper secondary schools with a shortage of teachers, schools with teachers transferring from other areas (especially female teachers), schools with long teaching hours and so on.

Seniority-based promotion

Promotion in the Cambodia public sector is largely based on seniority and working experience. Although there is no established in-service structured scheme that identifies high-potential officers in the Cambodia public sector, there is a separate scheme for in-service senior officials with a Ph.D. degree. These officials either have already attained a Ph.D. from elite schools or they are nominated by the respective ministries to be offered scholarships to pursue Ph.D. overseas. These scholarships are supported by either the government or a development partner such as United Nations Development Programme (UNDP), World Bank, ASEAN and so on. The officers will be bonded for 3 years to the current ministry upon completion and they will be promoted to director level or, at the highest, to the secretary of state level. After 3 years, they are free to move to other ministries and are bonded for another 2 years. Sponsored ad-hoc overseas training opportunities are also offered to these officers in accordance with the needs of the reforms – for example, the executive training programme sponsored by the Temasek Foundation. Since 2014, about 200 high-ranking officials including vice-ministers and director-generals from various ministries at central and provincial levels were sent to Singapore for executive training programmes at the Nanyang Centre for Public Administration. The 2-week training programme in collaboration with Cambodia's Ministry of Economics and Finance was conducted in both Phnom Penh and Singapore, straddling 1 week each, to equip them with the latest knowledge and skills to enhance their capabilities in the areas of governance and public sector management. Based on a preliminary survey conducted with about 30 alumni of the training programme at the Nanyang Centre for Public Administration, most of the trainees were promoted to the next level or an even higher level upon completion of the programme.

Reform of the civil service remuneration

In general, civil servants receive very low salaries and could not afford their living expenses with their wages in Cambodia (World Bank, 2013). Their pay level is lower than private companies' and even non-profit organisations'. The average salary of public officials was $75.5 in 2009 (Korm, 2011) which was still below subsistence level income for a family. Due to the widening of the gap between levels of state salaries and cost of living, public officials need to take up a second job, and this led to them paying less attention to their duties. Many civil servants work as a lecturer or consultant to earn extra income when they are off-duty. The low wage has also heightened corruption in the service and reduction in service performance. Although public officials in Custom and Taxation departments receive the same amount of salary as other public officials, they could receive more financial rewards based on the amount of tax income they collect. This is because the General Department of Taxation (GDT) does not receive the government budget, so the GDT could use 1.5 per cent of the tax revenue for its expenditure and provide some amount of money to their tax officials as a general reward. The amount is determined by their position and performance. Such an arrangement was also to reduce the level of corruption in the tax administration and encourage them to collect more taxes from the citizens. Such policy also closely models the pay for performance which is not being practiced in other domains in the civil service.

Responding to the low remuneration in the civil service, a substantial pay rise was announced in November 2020 for Prime Minister Hun Sen, Secretaries of state and 2,500 other civil servants and political figures after the Council of Ministers approved a draft of the 2017 Draft Law on Financial Management. The Prime Minister would treble from 3.6 million riels (about US$900) a month to 10 million (about US2,500). Ministers will receive 4.5 million riels (US$1,115), secretaries of state 3.5 million (about US$850), undersecretaries of state 2.8 million (US$700) and some 2,500 assistants and advisers will receive an extra 80,000 riels (US$20) a month. The Ministry of Education also announced that teachers' base salaries would rise to US$230 a month in April, up from US$193 at present (Socheath, 2020). While civil servants' pay should be competitive, when compared to the private sector, taking into account all additional benefits of civil service employment, including tenure of employment, learning and development opportunities, and status. At the same time, civil servants should also increase their productivity and performance.

7 Talent management and leadership development in Vietnam

Standardised development of cadres and civil servants

The 1986 Doi Moi reforms ('rejuvenation') initiated a broad-based economic transformation, which dismantled the largely planned economy (beginning with agricultural reforms), opened a closed economy to international markets and trade, and initiated pro-business reforms. These reforms were accompanied by a wide-ranging social agenda, led by an expansion of education and electricity, with a clear goal of 'leaving no one behind'. In the aftermath of these policies, Vietnam sustained high economic growth rates that catapulted the country from one of the poorest to a lower emerging market economy within 25 years (Khuong, 2015).

Since the start of Doi Moi, a number of initiatives have also been taken to improve the civil service legal framework towards fulfilling Vietnam's vision of a democratic, clean, strong and modernised civil service. Following the introduction of the Ordinance of Cadre and Civil Servants in 1998, policies and procedures for civil service management have been developed in a more systematic manner, compared with the previous period. The revision of the Ordinance on Cadre and Civil Servants in 2003 resulted in an improved classification and policies regarding the management of administrative civil servants and service delivery public officials. The promulgation of the national Public Administration Reform (PAR) Master Programme also (2001–2010) aims to develop a socialist rule of law state; a democratic, clean, strong, modernised and professionalised public administration; qualified and ethical cadres and civil servants; efficient and effective state agencies relevant to socialist-oriented market mechanism; and integration into the global economy to meet Vietnam's rapid and sustainable development.

The Vietnamese government has implemented various reform strategies in the public sectors, especially the public administrative procedures and public policies (Nguyen, 2006). However, one of the biggest challenges that Vietnam Reform would face was the limitation on managerial abilities of cadres and civil servants: some did not meet the needed innovative requirements;

some had strong manifestations of bureaucratic tendencies and territory that cause troubles to the people (Nguyen and Panganiban, 2000). Consequently, in 2008, Vietnam's Politburo decreed Project 165 'Training, fostering leaders, managers in foreign countries with the State's funding' to 'improve the capacity of leaders and managers in order to meet national demands of industrialization and modernization' (Project 165, 2008).

Even with the various reforms, the civil service management in Vietnam is still subject to many severe shortcomings such as poor human resource planning, bribery and frauds in the recruitment process, inadequate remuneration, unrealistic performance assessment, promotion not based on merit and systemic corruption. Whilst there have been training and development activities, the current contingent of civil servants still generally lacks the necessary competence, work ethics and motivation to meet the requirements of the country's development vision of industrialisation and modernisation. Furthermore, corruption is still common in the Vietnam civil service. The most common forms include soliciting bribes by creating obstacles, accepting bribes for favours and using public means for personal benefits. Low remuneration is often mentioned as the main reason for corruption in Vietnam; therefore, good human resource management practices that include human resource planning, transparent recruitment and promotion, training, compensation and performance appraisal are required.

Vietnam public sector

The Vietnam public sector is observed as a form of career-based system as there is no 'civil servant neutrality' with the communist party in Vietnam and the public sector. The officers are empowered by the State to perform the functions and duties of the State in the comprehensive management of all aspects of social life. In general, the regime of civil service and civil servants is a political-legal one largely dominated by politics. Civil servants enter the civil service in competitive recruitment and start their careers in the government system. A higher grade in the category in civil service has a great influence on career opportunities to be managers and leaders. The officers in the civil service are categorised as public officials and civil servants, public employees (Laws in 2008, 2011). The public officials are elected and appointed in fixed-term positions while civil servants are recruited and work in administrative agencies more or less on a permanent basis. Both categories of officers work in Party Organizations, Political Social Organizations and Administrative Agencies. The public employees are recruited to deliver public service.

Data from the General Statistics Office shows that at the end of 2017, there were more than 5.2 million people working in the Vietnam public sector. According to the World Bank, the size of Vietnam's public sector compared to the population is among the biggest in Southeast Asia. As provided by the data in 2017, there are 2,726,917 people working in the public sector. There are 611,069 Public Officials and Civil Servants, 1,983,981 officers working in public service deliveries. The civil servants are also categorised into four groups: Group A is senior experts, Group B is principle expert, Group C is expert, Group D is below expert. Each grouping category results in the promotion. It is normal for 9 years to jump the group.

The Ministry of Home Affairs (MOHA) is the main centralised agency for the management of the officers in Vietnam. MOHA performs the function of state management over the organisational and personnel fields of state agencies. The role of MOHA is to recommend the Government the right resolutions for strengthening the organisations of state administrative apparatus and cadres, civil servants and officials. MOHA also conducts and instructs or assists state administrative agencies in general to improve their organisations of administrative apparatus as well as their personnel staff.

Under the purview of MOHA, the Monitoring Office of Programme 165 (MOP165) is the leading national-level institution in Vietnam that is responsible for the training of government leaders and senior officials, focusing on political science and governance issues. The Ho Chi Minh National Academy of Politics and Public Administration (HCMA) is the national centre for training senior and middle-level leaders for the entire political system and Vietnamese state-owned corporations, as well as a research centre on political theory, science leadership and management of Vietnam. HCMA has contributed significantly to the development and international integration of Vietnam through training and educating high-level human resources for the country. The Academy has cooperative relations with nearly 200 international partners of more than 60 countries and territories. The Academy is the focal place to manage hundreds of cadres who were sent to do postdoctoral, doctoral or short-term training in the Soviet Union and Eastern European socialist countries.

Government scholarships

The Vietnam government keen to promote internationalisation has established a number of scholarship programmes to fund undergraduate and postgraduate studies to groom public sector officials. The various scholarships are summarised in Table 7.1.

The scholarship mainly covers the tuition fees, e.g., the 911 project, launched in 2013, is slated to fund 10,000 Ph.D. candidates to study abroad until 2020 with up to USD $15,000 annually per student. The scholarships

Table 7.1 Summary of scholarships offered by the respective agencies in Vietnam

S/N	Scholarship Programme	Type of Scholarship	Executive Agency	Scholarship Programme Brief	Selection Criteria	English Level	Field of Study
1	Project 911	Postgraduate	Ministry of Education and Training	To produce 20,000 doctoral degree holders for tertiary institutions by 2020, of which: – 10,000 students for overseas doctoral programmes – 3,000 students for sandwich doctoral programmes – 10,000 students for in-country doctoral programmes	– Academic staff from tertiary institutions (universities and colleges) – Research fellows of research institutes – Graduates with high GPA (over 70 per cent of 100 point scale); and non-academic staff who are professional capable and competent and commit to become and wish to be academic staff for tertiary institutions after training	– Requirement for pre-selection: 5.5 IELTS or TOEFL equivalent – Up to admission requirements of host institutions for unconditional letters of offer for the chosen courses	All study fields with priorities in Engineering, Technology, Environment, Agriculture, BioTechnology etc.
2	Project 599	Undergraduate and Masters	Ministry of Education and Training	– Programme offers 30 undergraduate awards and about 330 awards for master's degrees annually – Around 220 awardees will be sent to Australia for Master and undergraduate levels – The project includes funding for Master's sandwich programmes in similar study areas where international lectures teach in Vietnam	– Under 45 years of age – Top high-school graduates for undergraduate studies – Forty per cent of master's awards are for public servants	– Requirement for pre-selection: 5.5 IELTS or TOEFL equivalent – Up to admission requirements of host institutions for unconditional letters of offer for the chosen courses	The area of studies will be those areas not available in Vietnam, such as cybersecurity, nanotechnology, new material science, climate change, and post-harvest technology

(Continued)

Table 7.1 (Continued)

S/N	Scholarship Programme	Type of Scholarship	Executive Agency	Scholarship Programme Brief	Selection Criteria	English Level	Field of Study
3	Programme 165	Short course and postgraduate	Central Committee of the Communist Party of Vietnam	To provide overseas training at the postgraduate level and short course training for government officers and talented graduates to strengthen the human resources capacity of the country	For Ph.D.: under 40 years old, have Master's degree related to the field of study For Master: under 35, have Bachelor's degree at a good level	– Up to admission requirements of host institutions for unconditional letters of offer for the chosen courses – Project 165 organises and funds in-country English training course for eligible candidates who have not met English requirement of host institutions	Administrative management; Economics management; Environment management; Urban management; Social management; International law; Justice; Public service, IT etc.

awarded by the Vietnamese Ministry of Education are predominantly given to students going to Russia. Only the Project 599 scholarship programme is catered for high school graduates while the rest are all for in-service officials in various domains. However, it is not clear whether the candidates will be required to work in the public sector upon completion of their undergraduate studies. Looking at the fields of studies, it seems to suggest that they will join the service for these new domains as Vietnam embarks on the next stage of development. Proficiency in English is one of the criteria as English is not the primary language in Vietnam.

International aided scholarships

There are also various scholarships that are offered by International organisations; one of such is the Project for Human Resource Development Scholarship (JDS). This is also for in-service officers. The Project for Human Resource Development Scholarship (JDS) is a grant aid project conducted by Japan International Cooperation Agency (JICA) that provides scholarships to international students from partner governments. It started in Vietnam in 2000 and up to the present, there is a total of 691 fellows who have been sent to Japan. Within the new framework of 2018–2021, JDS provides 2-year master courses in various study fields including Economics, Urban Development/Transport, Energy, Agriculture, Environment, Legal System, and Public Administration at Japanese universities. The JDS programme, formerly Japanese Grant Aid for Human Resource Development Scholarship (JDS), provides full scholarship including tuition fee, flight tickets, monthly scholarship, and other allowances funded by the government of Japan through official development assistance (ODA). JDS fellows are also expected to contribute to the enhanced bilateral relations between their countries and Japan, with a well-rounded knowledge of Japan.

Recruitment and training

Vietnam's public employment system had undergone drastic policy changes and achieved certain successes such as standardising and decentralising recruitment and promotion of public employees in the Home Affairs sector, doubling civil service wages, granting greater autonomy to agencies in relation to recruitment and wage policies and expanding the enrolments in training institutions of public administrations (Hausman, 2010). The recruitment has been changed towards the merit-based selection methods. All public officials and civil servants and public employees are recruited and promoted through competitive examinations. The recruitment is internal and decentralised to line ministries and localities in provinces and cities including the public service deliveries. The recruitment criterion focuses mainly on fairness, openness and objectiveness which is difficult to uphold due to nepotism. However, competitive examination was not appropriate for selecting the best candidates due to the irrelevant and outdated methods and the examination questions are not designed to assess the best candidates by their knowledge and skills, especially the soft skills which cannot be evaluated through written examinations. In addition, the examination process also cannot stop fraud and bribery such as 'buying posts' and 'buying degree' (Top Summit of Political Report of 10th CPV Congress).

There are no special schemes for leadership development in the Vietnam public sector, maybe because of its close link to the communist party. The establishment of the working position-based civil service already determined in the Law on Cadres and Civil Servants and Law on Public Employees remains too cautious, partly due to the inertness of the old career-based civil service. The training for civil servants was undifferentiated and limited. The training curriculums are mainly for politics and state management which are designed to meet the common knowledge required for the experts, principal experts, and not relevant for the daily jobs. The training needs assessment is rarely carried out in all types of training courses, so the training programmes are often ineffective to fill in the capacity gaps of the civil servants and public employees. The political dimension of training is often paid higher attention more than the professional skills, rather than the development of soft skills. The training and development for public employees also do not address the capacity building of the public sector to offer quality public services.

In recent years, the emphasis of training of civil servants in Vietnam is moving towards specific groups such as the teachers and the civil servants of the Home Affairs.

Pre- and in-service training programme for teachers

The government recognised that educating only the young would be insufficient to lift sufficient people out of poverty in the short term, given the longer lag of school children entering the labour market. As result, education for both the young as well as the out-of-school population was strengthened. In 1992, Vietnam agreed on the 'Education For All' (EFA) 1993 to 2000 Action Plan, followed by a second EFA for 2003–2015, to provide primary education for all, gender equality across all levels of education, and appropriate education and training for all out-of-school young people and adults. Therefore, providing support to teachers was a cornerstone of the education reform. The teachers and educational managers were regarded as the leading decisive factors in ensuring high-quality and effective education (EFA, 2003; Parandekar and Sedmik, 2016). The development of new pre- and in-service training programmes was initiated at a massive scale for all teachers so that the quality of education can be improved.

Ministry of Home Affairs (MOHA)

Civil servants of MOHA in Vietnam refer to those working in the executive, legislative and judicial public branches of the state and municipal government and are responsible for a wide range of state and local government administration, education and training, emulation and reward, state management of religions, archiving, and youth development affairs (The Government of Vietnam, 2017a). Vietnamese civil servants of MOHA play a critical role in advising the Government of Vietnam on policies related to the management and development of the whole public administration system (Cuong, 2019). To improve the performance of officials and cadres, specific training and retraining programmes for Vietnamese civil servants of Home Affairs have been catered for them.

The training and retraining of civil servants of MOHA are being implemented in accordance with the Government's Decree No. 101/2017/NĐ-CP dated 1/9/2017 on the training and retraining of officials and civil servants (The Government of Vietnam, 2017b) and the Ministry of Home Affairs' Circular No. 01/2018/TT-BNV dated 8/1/2018 on the training and retraining of civil servants of Home Affairs (Vietnam Ministry of Home Affairs, 2018). Training and retraining programmes mainly focus on improving professional skills and knowledge, managerial skills, and political understanding for civil servants of different positions, ranks and grades.

Wage increment and performance appraisal

The salary system is a great challenge for human resource management in the government of Vietnam. Each position or grade on a salary scale consists of 9 levels, and each level is rooted by the minimum salary and salary scale. The cadre and civil servant salary in the scales is simply multiplied by the minimum salary to salary scale. However, the salary does not cover the cost of living, so officers often depend on other income sources which include running side businesses. Taking bribes has also become a good income source. The Vietnamese National Assembly (NA) on 12 November 2019 approved a government proposal to raise wages for civil servants by 7.3 per cent from July 1, 2020 (Baum, 2020). Accordingly, the monthly base wages of civil servants and public employees will be hiked from VND1.49 million (US$64) per month to VND1.6 million (US$69) per month. This will be the boldest wage hike in the past 8 years. The previous wage raise was a 7.2 per cent hike, effective from 1 July 2019. The pensions, social insurance allowances, prescribed monthly allowances and preferential allowances will also be adjusted for officers with meritorious services in accordance with the base wage increase.

The performance appraisal did not work well in the government of Vietnam as the eight criteria applied for all cadres and civil servants. Without the distinction, it is not able to assess the performance of the cadre and civil servants fairly and accurately especially since the job scope and description are different and so it is difficult to evaluate performance accordingly. The performance appraisal system is also just a paper exercise that does not provide performance-related incentives and so it also does not encourage and motivate the officers to perform.

8 Comparison of the talent management practices – attraction, development and retention

Comparison of talent management strategies through attraction, development and retention stages

Deployment of talent management strategies can be generally classified into three main stages as in Figure 8.1.

Talent attraction

Pre-service scholarship

All five countries offer scholarships to high-school graduates; however, not all countries offer careers in the service to scholarship recipients upon completion of their studies. Among these four countries, Singapore is the most successful in adopting the scholarship system as a talent attraction strategy. It has the most comprehensive and diverse offering of fields from general to specialisation and provides well-planned and differentiated scholarships that cater to different domains including uniform and non-uniform groups which guarantee employment upon completion of their studies. The recipients will be bonded from 4 to 6 years. The statutory boards also offer specialised scholarships to groom individuals in specific domains in line with the country's development stage. Cambodia offers two types of scholarships, one of which is only offered to eligible teacher-candidates and they will serve as teachers in the rural areas upon completion. Another type is for officers entering the Grade A scheme (senior official grade) who graduated from elite universities to be offered scholarships to pursue a Ph.D. at local and overseas universities. As for Thailand, the two main scholarships namely the King's Scholarship and Royal Thai Government Scholarship are not specific to any domains and are allocated upon agencies' requirements. Recipients also must serve the public service upon completion of their studies with twice the amount of time taken to study. Unlike Singapore or Cambodia, they are not placed in special schemes; therefore, due to the lack of prior

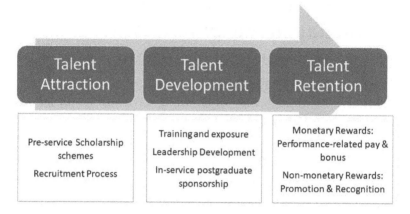

Figure 8.1 Talent management practices corresponding to the three talent management stages

planning, they might be allocated to areas that are not of their expertise. For scholarship recipients from Malaysia, they are not guaranteed job in the service and the types have also been broadened to include diploma studies as well. In addition, for the scholarships to fund overseas degrees in generic fields such as Arts, Business and Islamic Studies, they have been converted to loans and will be made repayable upon graduation. This is likely in response to the possibility that the returnees might not be able to obtain a career in the public sector to serve their bonds. They are also encouraged to take up jobs in the private sector after a year if there are still no suitable positions for them in the service. As for Vietnam, the scholarships are only offered to areas of studies not available in Vietnam, such as cybersecurity, nanotechnology, new material science, climate change and post-harvest technology. Recipients will likely join the service in preparation for the knowledge-based economy but it is not clear if they will be bonded.

Recruitment drive

Singapore, Malaysia and Thailand practice open recruitments for different grades and schemes of services as and when there are vacancies or new positions. For Singapore and Malaysia, both fresh graduates and mid-career switchers are encouraged to apply, while for Thailand, positions are only open to fresh graduates. Recruitments in Singapore and Malaysia are throughout the year and available positions are made accessible to the public via government job portals. Applications are also made via the job portals. For Singapore, the list of job openings and respective hiring agencies will be made available in the portal and interested individuals will apply in accordance with their choices. For Malaysia, the job portal will job-match the applicants and offer them the most suitable posts based on the requirements and educational backgrounds. The hiring process in Singapore is decentralised as the respective hiring agencies will proceed with the subsequent shortlisting, interviewing and selection stages. For Malaysia, successfully shortlisted candidates who have gone through interviews will need to take examinations before they are appointed. In responding to the job market needs, a short-term contract-based employment has also been introduced in 2021 to fresh graduates via apprenticeship. Malaysia is also opening up more opportunities for non-Malay applicants, a step forward to shift from its Bumiputera-based civil service. For Thailand, as there is a need to control the number of officers in the service, recruitment is not throughout the year and there are three routes to enter service. The first is through competitive examination, second is by selection from respective hiring agencies to fill up vacancies, and third is through special appointment authorised by CSC. On the other hand, recruitment and availability of positions are not made publicly available in Cambodia and Vietnam. In Cambodia, only those who have close links in the service will know about vacancies. The number of positions to be filled is decided on a bloc basis and each agency will submit their required number of positions and once approved, they can proceed to recruit. Fresh school leavers and graduates will be required to take the entrance examinations while contract workers who wished to be converted to full-time staff and mid-career switchers are exempted from taking the examination. As for Vietnam, recruitment is internal, and candidates will also need to take examinations in order to enter the service. Among the countries, Singapore is the only country that does not require candidates to take generic examinations that might not provide an evaluation of whether candidates are fit for the positions. Singapore adopted other evaluation methods including scrutiny of candidates' educational background, confirmation from referees, psychometric assessments and any other form of tests as stipulated by respective hiring agencies which are appropriate for the position, e.g., writing of policy recommendation pertaining to the domain or sector.

Talent development

Training and exposure

All five countries offer adequate training opportunities to all officers. There are also dedicated organisations such as the respective public service divisions (Singapore, Malaysia and Thailand) or ministries (Cambodia and Vietnam) that oversee the training and development needs of the officers. They will also collaborate with training providers and institutions, locally and overseas to design appropriate courses to cater to the demands of the public service. All officers in Singapore public sector are granted with annual 100 training hours which shows the dedication for officers to upgrade themselves constantly. All the five countries also have central training institutions that officers can attend courses; however, not all the institutions have their in-house faculty. For Singapore and Cambodia, the courses are taught by associate trainers who are subject matter experts either within the service or from other sectors. Besides training, these institutions also conduct research on governance and public administration topics to share best practices. INTAN is also responsible for developing and conducting assessments. Officers in Singapore are encouraged to participate in different cross-team/department/agency projects to gain exposure and also to network with peers beyond their department and agency. In addition, all officers in Singapore will also get to experience different jobs as they are being rotated within the agencies even if they do not belong to any of the leadership development schemes. In Thailand, in recognition of the low ICT literacy rate of the civil servants, a new, large-scale training programme has been implemented to increase the digital literacy and ICT proficiency of public servants across the country. Similar training that focuses on digital government and public sector innovations is also initiated to train civil servants. Like many of its scholarship schemes, this initiative is also sponsored by its close developmental partner, UNDP. While Vietnam offers uniform training for all cadres and civil servants, there are also designated training programmes designed for all teachers and civil servants of MOHA. The objectives of this training are to equip the knowledge and skills of these two groups so that they can improve their work performance and deliver quality service.

Leadership development

There are specific leadership development schemes in Singapore, Malaysia and Thailand. These are generally known as fast-track scheme pathways to groom selected high-performance or high-potential officers to attain leadership positions. For Singapore, there are two pathways, namely, generalist and specialist in ministries. For the generalist pathway, officers will become AOs, finally assuming roles as Permanent Secretaries or Deputy Secretaries in ministries while for the specialist pathway, apex positions include Director of Medical Services, or the Director-General of Education, or the Chief Planner, the Accountant-General or Chief of Government

Communications. There are also the various MAPs offered by statutory boards which expose new officers to different areas within a short term of 12 months to groom them to take on leadership roles in the respective agencies. For Malaysia, the ADS groom new officers to assume the role of senior civil servants who are generalist and involved in all stages of policy formulation and its implementation while the Fast-Track scheme provides opportunities for in-service officers to be exposed to different jobs through rotations and faster promotion opportunities. For Thailand, unlike Singapore and Malaysia that offer fast-track advancement, the three schemes – PSED, HiPPS and NWLDP – provide overseas training opportunities and private secondments to gain diverse and international exposure. These schemes are more to equip and prepare the officers in their skills, knowledge and exposure for their future career progression in the service.

In-service postgraduate sponsorship

Singapore and Vietnam are the only countries that offer in-service officers with opportunity and sponsorship to further their studies without an appointment in a leadership scheme, while the rest of the three countries only offer such opportunities to specific individuals appointed to the leadership development schemes or to the highest grade of service. In Singapore, officers can enrol in a formal postgraduate degree of their choice, and support from the parent agency can be in the form of unrecorded leave or sponsorship of course fees. For sponsorship of course fees, officers will be bonded upon completion. As for Vietnam, there are several postgraduate or short-course scholarships that officers can choose from. Officers will be assessed on the basis of the respective criteria as specified for each programme and will be selected accordingly within the established quota. In Cambodia, only senior officers with qualifications from elite universities, appointed in the grade A scheme are offered scholarships to pursue a Ph.D. Many of these scholarships in Cambodia are sponsored by developmental partners such as ADB. Upon completion of their studies, they will be designated as deputy (under-secretary) or heads (secretary) of ministries. In Malaysia, officers nominated to the fast-track scheme can also be offered study sponsorships for higher education at the master's or doctoral levels. However, they are not guaranteed higher positions upon completion of their studies or assignments. It is not specified in Thailand if postgraduate studies are sponsored for in-service officers but officers in specific schemes are sent for short-term overseas courses in different countries. These courses are sponsored by OCSC and respective parent agencies.

Talent retention

Monetary rewards: performance-related pay and bonus

Singapore has created a system of flexible compensation that is linked to performance. This allows for a variety of pay scales for the civil service, including those identified and earmarked to be groomed as leaders. For example, the Administrative officers have a different pay scale that is much higher. This is not the case for the rest of the four countries. However, there are attempts being made to change the remuneration system for civil servants hoping to be comparable to the private sector. So far, Singapore is the only country among the five that closely links pay increments and bonuses in accordance with individual performance. There is also a special bonus offered to the civil servants (but not officers in statutory boards) which is tied to the performance of the country's economy. For Malaysia, the new performance evaluation scheme has allowed more flexibility in deciding the pay increment of individual officers so that the wage increment can relate to individuals' performance. The country continues its ongoing efforts to improve the remuneration system to provide a higher range of increment for officers from different grades. In the move towards rewarding officers' performance, Malaysia has introduced a one-time special bonus/financial incentive to members of the federal civil service who are serving in the states of Perak, Sarawak and Penang and Thailand has created a bonus-like scheme that reward only the senior officers. As for Cambodia and Vietnam, civil servants are struggling with the critically low wage which cannot cover the living expenditures and has led to systemic corruption, moonlighting and officers engage in other forms of businesses. Although recommendations are being made to improve the wage structure, it will take time for the situations to improve in both countries.

Non-monetary rewards: promotion and recognition

Even though Singapore has completely moved away from the seniority-based promotion system, the promotion of officers is not only based on performance but on potential as well. The potential of the officers is determined by the CEP which is based on competencies such as educational merits, intellectual and leadership qualities, and decide when the officer should enter the service. The scholars are usually rated with higher CEP scores based on this criterion and therefore will be promoted faster than the rest of the officers. This implies that the AOs will become top leaders at a relatively young age while experienced non-AOs are lagging behind.

For the rest of the four countries, promotion is still largely seniority based; only officers in specific fast-track schemes, e.g., PTD in Malaysia can skip grades/levels and progress at a faster rate than their peers in the generic career schemes. For Vietnam and Cambodia, many civil service servants are also promoted after they have attended overseas leadership programme while Thailand still values seniority and experience when it comes to promotions.

Talent management strategy at the different development stages

Even though all the five countries have similar talent management practices to attract, develop and retain talents, in comparison, Singapore has the most comprehensive and matured talent management strategy that not only enables individual growth but inculcates innovation and networks with well-established performance management systems coupled with training and rotations. This also coincides with it being the only developed country in the Southeast Asia region and at the advanced stage of development compared to the rest of the four countries. Singapore, now having a relatively stable economy, focuses more on developing its officers to be specialists in respective sectors to be ready for future challenges and uncertainties including 'black swan' events like the COVID-19 pandemic. Especially in the area of ICT, the Singapore government is attracting and grooming a pool of deep technological talent and leaders by offering the Smart Nation Scholarship.

The approach to talent management of officers in Malaysia and Thailand is similar, focusing more on exposures internationally through training and engagements with overseas partners and closer relationships with the private sector. This also aligns with their similar stage of development towards becoming high-middle income countries and also en-route to digitising public services and towards Smart Nations (as we also see many Smart Nation initiative collaborations between Malaysia and China as well as E-commerce development in Thailand). Especially for Thailand, as central agencies are instrumental in the formation and implementation of e-government strategies in the country, it is launching wide-scale ICT training for all levels of civil servants throughout the country to improve their digital literacy and ICT proficiency.

Cambodia and Vietnam are still developing countries with more concentration on their economic growth, urban development to improve infrastructures, industrialisation and resolving corruption in the service. Much like Singapore at the stage when it first achieved independence and the governments are more focused on their economies than the development of their officers. Improving the quality of education is the highest priority for Cambodia and Vietnam and so there are schemes to develop teachers at pre- and in-service. While in Vietnam, priority is on industrialisation and urban developments. As the integrity of the service and corruption issues are still serious in the country, there are still ongoing reforms towards resolving corruption issues and improving public services.

The structure of the government is a perspective that should be taken into observation as the structure of authority of responsible agencies is an important factor to explain the scope of talent development that each government draws. Thailand's OCSC and OPDC only oversee civil servants in the mainline ministries and not government-linked corporations and independent agencies. Due to the limited rotation possibilities, officers on HiPPS scheme or PSED do not have the opportunity to cross-train beyond service. This is very different in Singapore, where PSC and PSD, through the whole-of-government approach, can provide rotation to many types of public organisations, thereby giving civil service officers ample exposure to difficult tasks including a secondment to statutory boards and government-linked companies. The close relationship between the Malaysian civil service and the GLCs has also facilitated cross-sector postings for the officers in the Fast-Track scheme. Public training institutions also play an integral role in the design and development of training curriculum and programmes. Singapore's Civil Service College (CSC) and Malaysia's INTAN not only play an integrated role to execute training programmes, but they are also involved in public administration research to further inform best practices to the officers through the various types of training conducted through subject matter experts. Vietnam's Ho Chi Minh National Academy of Politics and Public Administration (HCMA) is the national centre for training. But unlike CSC and INTAN, it only provided training for senior and middle-level leaders for the entire political system and Vietnamese state-owned corporations. In Thailand, besides the Civil Service Training Institute (CSTI) which oversees and conducts training for the central administration and King Prajadhipok's Institute (KPI) which conducts training for all levels of officers (including provincial), the OCSC also coordinates and organises overseas training for officers in HiPPS. Cambodia however does not have a training institution; training is coordinated through Economics and Finance Institute (EFI) but only in Public Economics and Financial Management. EFI also collaborates with overseas institutions to organise training for senior-level officials.

Singapore, having gone through all the similar stages of development and being able to achieve developed status rapidly, has been highly regarded by its neighbouring countries as the model to learn from especially its lessons and experiences on overcoming all the challenges when it achieved independence in the 1960s. The emphasis on leadership development has also moved away from the pragmatic command and control environment towards a more facilitative and consultative network environment. However, taking account of the uniqueness of Singapore's political situation and size, its model of talent management cannot be transplanted wholesale to the participants' countries because of economic, administrative, cultural, operational and other differences. While some aspects of Singapore's talent schemes and performance management system can be adopted, it should not be modelled after completely. Nevertheless, it can contribute towards our understanding of talent management as a framework to develop a future-ready public sector.

9 Leadership development of senior public officials through transnational knowledge transfer

Knowledge sharing and transfer as part of leadership development

Knowledge transfer is the process of sharing tacit and explicit knowledge between two agents and its success is associated with the ability to recreate transferred knowledge in a new context (Kumar & Ganesh, 2009). Knowledge sharing and transfer has since developed into an important pillar of development cooperation based on the notion of 'sharing experience' within the countries which is derived from certain geographical characteristics, socio-cultural similarities or practical knowledge gained from the developing years (UNDP, 2016). Besides looking to other political systems for knowledge and ideas about institutions, programmes and policies, developing countries have also found overseas training to be an effective and efficient way to improve their public administrators' skills and expertise (Commons, 2012). The senior civil servants especially played a significant role in the development of the country and therefore as part of leadership development, learning from the experiences of other administrations is an integral element of leadership development and as we have seen is a component in the talent schemes. Hence, the education and training of public officials overseas have become a powerful mechanism for policy learning and transfer through the bringing back of international 'know-how' and good practice (Common, 2012).

Effective transnational knowledge transfer for overseas training is the process in which knowledge about policies, administrative arrangements or institutions are recreated and translated into specific projects, initiatives and changes in mindset. It is a key to success in a world undergoing accelerating globalisation and technological advancement as continue learn and adjust in order for their countries to survive and succeed in an era of intense competition, global connectivity and rapid technological change which led to countries learning from one another. The fundamental purpose of training is the effective transfer of relevant knowledge and skills to the workplace, which may vary according to the enabling organisational characteristics (Lim & Morris, 2006; Newcomer et al., 2010). A government-endorsed organisational commitment that matches training needs with strategic goals, and allows the proper transfer of acquired knowledge and skills, would ultimately increase the opportunity for success of capacity-building programmes (Adetunji, 2012; Lim & Morris, 2006; Majeed, 2010; Meyer-Sahling, 2011; Nakrošis, 2014; Newcomer et al., 2010; OECD, 2017; Rondineli, 2004).

Policy learning and transfer through transnational training of senior civil servants

As we have witnessed from the various leadership development schemes in Singapore, Malaysia, Thailand and Cambodia, officers are sent for overseas visits, training and short stints. Learning from overseas is not a new activity for policymakers. Since the birth of the state, officials have sought to learn the positive and negative lessons from their counterparts elsewhere (Evans, 2009). Over the past two decades or so, technological advances in air travelling and communications have further deepened the pool of policy know-how available and increased the occurrences of transfer. In addition, pressures exerted by global, social and economic forces produce common policy problems and an incentive to find and share common policy solutions (Bennett, 1991, Drezner, 2001, Holzinger & Knill, 2005).

Transnational training of public senior civil servants had therefore become a powerful mechanism for policy learning and transfer (Common, 2012). Transnational knowledge transfer includes knowledge transfer activities and transnational training for policy officials that promote diagnostic coordination across policy communities and developing countries (Broome & Seabrooke, 2015). It is important that when governments learn from other countries, it is in the public interest as a new or altered policy can affect the fabric of the society (Legrand, 2012). The study of policy transfer is 'a theory of policy development that seeks to make sense of a process or set of processes in which knowledge about institution, policies or delivery systems at one sector or level of governance is used in the development of institutions, policies or delivery systems at another sector or level of governance' (Evans, 2009, pp. 243–244). In broad terms, policy transfer is initiated by jurisdictions, international organisations, agencies etc. in order to develop a policy that addresses a particular policy issue/problem (Dolowitz & Marsh, 2012).

In lesson-drawing, learning occurs via transnational 'epistemic communities' and takes the view that learning takes place in 'complex arrangements of state and societal actors in various types of domestic and transnational

policy networks and communities'. Learning only takes place when policymakers modify policies in the light of knowledge gained, so in policy
convergence or harmonisation, learning can lead to the development of
'consensual knowledge' about the functioning of state and society experienced at similar development stages taking place in different countries
even if there is no direct link between them. Consequently, policy diffusion
arises through independent actions by policymakers. The emphasis is on
the learning process and the conditions for absorption of knowledge rather
than the content. Finally, policy transfer connotes learning that results in
a more coherent transfer of ideas, policies and practices when there is a
consensus among actors inside and outside government to introduce new
ideas. The contemporary study of policy transfer originates from policy
diffusion studies that focus on identifying trends in timing, geography
and resource similarities in the diffusion of innovations between countries
(Dolowitz & Marsh, 2000; Benson & Jordan, 2011; Evans, 2017). Hence,
knowledge transfer at the transnational level implies a direct exchange process between exporting and importing countries.

Like most developing countries in the world, Southeast Asia has experienced a long history of development cooperation. Under the impact of
the Western colonial legacies, Southeast Asian countries are attracted to the
development of the European and American knowledge, which led to countries in Southeast Asia sending public officials overseas for policy learning
and transfer through the bringing back of international 'know-how' and
good practice (Common, 2012; Duan et al., 2006; Jessop & Sum, 2000).
Besides looking to other political systems for knowledge and ideas about
institutions, programmes and policies, developing countries have also found
overseas training to be an effective and efficient way to improve their public administrators' skills and expertise (Sun & Ross, 2009). This included
Singapore during the developing years in the 1950s, which was also a beneficiary of learning abroad from developed countries such as Germany and
the Netherlands. Singapore in the postcolonial and post-independence day
was struck with a high unemployment rate and weak economy with many
social challenges. The Singapore government not only received help and
advice from the United Nations Development Programme (UNDP), its
predecessors and sister agencies UNDP, 2,029 officers from the Singapore
administration (many of whom are of Singapore's best and brightest) were
awarded fellowships from 1950 to 1985 by UNDP and related UN agencies to study abroad and work on UNDP projects. Among the fellows was
Mr. Ong Teng Cheong, one of Singapore's former presidents, who was
then a government architect seconded to the UNDP project on urban
planning on transport and land use. Mr. Ong had also received a Colombo
Plan to study urban planning at the University of Liverpool. In addition,

many officers were also provided grants to study abroad in Japan and Germany (GCPSE, 2015). The success of Singapore was very much due to Dr. Albert Winsemius, a Dutch economist, policymaker and also United Nations advisor who worked very closely with the Singapore government to take a pragmatic approach to assume the role of a facilitator to fuel economic and industrial development by opening up its economy even though the rest of the countries in the region was practising nationalisation policy. It led to the establishment of non-political bodies or statutory boards in specific areas of commerce and industry like the Economic Development Board (EDB), Development Bank of Singapore (DBS), Jurong Town Corporation (JTC), Port Authority of Singapore. The Singapore government also strengthened the foundations of tripartite relations among the Government, employers and workers which leads to industrial peace and economic growth. Dr. Winsemius also invited several multinational companies such as Shell, Esso and Philips to invest in Singapore. The CEP which determines the potential of respective civil servants that we have seen in the previous chapter on Singapore was a concept adopted from Shell. Therefore, Singapore Government had always been a strong advocate of learning from overseas and adapting models and ideas into its own context.

The year 1955 marked a time of large-scale efforts to export the Weberian's model of public administration from the United States of America into Europe, Asia, Latin America and Africa, institutionalised through training, education, research and professional association (Siffin, 1976). Since 1958, the University of Manchester has been training public administrators from developing countries such as India and Thailand (Clarke, 1999). Many of the officials who trained from these countries returned to implement these western New Public Management ideologies. In the recent two to three decades, there has been a shift of overseas training and learning from North-South to South-South as the North-South transfer has met with challenges due to the disparity in levels of state capacity between developed and developing countries and cultural misfit (Barcham, 2003). After the decline of the developed economies in the USA and Europe in the late 1990s and the 2000s, the era of one-way North-South assistance has become outdated, especially with the emergence of Japan's economy.

Shifting of learning from the West to Asia to within Asia

The idea of 'sharing experience' within the region of East and Southeast Asia became clearer with the establishment of the Manila-based network secretariat of the Konrad-Adenauer-Stiftung (KAS) and Local Government Development Foundation. In 1997, six countries including Indonesia,

Korea, Malaysia, the Philippines, Thailand and Vietnam participated as cooperating partners. In 2000, based on their in-depth site studies, they published two books emphasising the idea of the 'East and Southeast Asian Network for better Local Government' which contributes to make best-practice examples of the so-called New Public Management available as models that may be adopted in other local authorities and countries. During the 1997–1998 Economy crisis, Japan was by far the single most important provider of assistance to East Asian and Southeast Asian economies. Japan's economic miracle aroused great interest among world leaders and industrialists who were keen to know how Japan had made it and what was its winning formula. Ezra Vogel's book, Japan as Number One (1979) was a timely release that soon contributed to the rush in America, as well as Southeast Asian countries, to learn from Japan. It was inevitable for Singapore to be among those who jumped on the bandwagon of the 'learn from Japan' drive and encourage Singaporeans to study in Japan as a way to build up a base of locals with sound knowledge of the country. Concern for productivity as such in the civil service and the nation also prompted Malaysia to launch the 'Look East Policy' focusing attention on Japan and Korea as a model for development, sending students to be trained in Japan and through working on joint venture enterprises with Japan. However, with the advent of a slow or zero or negative growth rate of the Japanese economy after the crises, Japan ceased to be a magnet to East and Southeast Asia.

Learning within Asia has become an important modality for the capacity building of public officials. The exchanges of this nature have increased substantially in recent years hosted by the more successful neighbours to facilitate knowledge, skills expertise and resource sharing. These pivot host countries include Singapore, Malaysia, China, Brunei, India and Brazil. The experience of these more successful countries can help countries in transitioning to middle-income status through training and skills development.

Phenomenon of Southeast Asia public sector leaders attending leadership training and development in Singapore

Due to the geographical proximity, shared histories and cultures, Singapore's emergence as a newly industrialised economy caught the attention of its Southeast Asian neighbours and they are looking to Singapore which is the forerunner that has overcome these challenges for a solution. As a beneficiary of overseas learnings, Singapore recognises the importance of institutional and human resource capacity building in a nation's development. It has since been sharing and transferring its developmental experience with countries around the world in Asia, Africa, Middle East, Eastern Europe and Latin America (Saxena, 2011). As part of SSC, the Ministry of Foreign Affairs established the Singapore Cooperation Programme (SCP) in 1992 to provide training especially to Cambodia, Laos, Myanmar and Vietnam (CLMV countries) and also small island developing states. More than 115,000 officials from about 170 countries such as China, Southeast and South Asian nations (Saxena, 2011) have benefitted from the programme. These training programmes are offered directly on a government-to-government basis (Bilateral Programmes) or in partnership with a developed country or organisation (Third Country Training Programmes) through its training partners and agencies such as the Civil Service College International (CSCI), United Nations Developing Programme (UNDP) and higher educational institutions like Nanyang Technological University (NTU) and National University of Singapore (NUS). Furthermore, under the Initiative for ASEAN Integration (IAI), Singapore has pledged about SG$170 million to provide human resource capacity building development to the CLMV countries. Singapore has also established training centres in each CLMV country to conduct training in areas ranging from the English language to public administration. In 2018, these centres were upgraded to Singapore Cooperation Centres to boost regional economic integration and adoption of technology. As of October 2018, 1,900 programmes have been conducted at the four centres, with over 39,000 government officials having participated in classroom-style courses.

Governments in ASEAN recognise the need to strengthen public service institutions and civil service as essential for achieving the ASEAN Vision 2025 when their reforms have been met with varying degrees of success and challenges (OECD, 2019; ASEAN, 2017). For instance, countries such as Cambodia, Myanmar, Thailand and Vietnam are still working on their transformation into corruption-free, ethical, merit-based organisations (ASEAN, 2017). Singapore's well-known profile as one of the world's most competitive countries (ranked first in 2019) and least corrupted countries (ranked 4th in Corruption Perception index 2019) is contributed by its good governance, high-quality infrastructure, economic performance and social and political stability (Quah, 2013; Liu & Wang, 2018). Being one of the founding members of ASEAN, Singapore is always keen to disseminate best practices and share experiences. Singapore also hopes to maintain diplomacy with other countries through the programmes and become a transmitter of culture and political ideas to generate soft power for the state, endowing it with standing and influence above its physical size (Lee, 2015; Henderson, 2012; Saxena, 2011).

Singapore's success can be attributed to its excellent public administrative model and system (Quah, 2018). Training in the Singapore public sector is integral to the country's success and has established a career training roadmap for its administrative officers (Poocharoen & Lee, 2013). The emphasis on meritocracy and training in Singapore's public bureaucracy has resulted in a high level of competence of the personnel in implementing policies (Jones, 2016). Training is embedded in its administrative structure and socio-cultural and political milieu that contributes to the country's successes and its resilience against external threats (Lee & Rezaei, 2019; Neo & Chen, 2007; Quah, 1996). Bilateral leadership programmes such as ASEAN Border Leadership Exchange Programme and Leaders in Governance Programme have been designed and organised annually by SCP to distil and exchange knowledge and experiences among senior public officials. There are also various public agencies and higher educational institutions offering structured leadership training programmes for senior officials in Southeast Asia and beyond.

Outcome from leadership development programmes: cases from Nanyang Centre for Public Administration

Effective leadership and good governance are critical factors for the success of a nation. Hence, leadership training is an essential and strategic component of development plans for public sector managers. Unlike the private sector, there are several features of the public sector that act as constraints on a leader's ability to lead and be effective, which diminish or even neutralise the impact of leadership on followers and organisations (Seidle et al., 2016). Hence, training interventions unique to the public sector are a necessity for leaders to adeptly navigate the complex political, legal and organisational environment and to lead their subordinates and organisations effectively.

Many middle- to senior-level officials from Thailand, Cambodia and Vietnam had also attended customised short-term executive training programmes in the Nanyang Centre for Public Administration (NCPA), Nanyang Technological University (during 2014 to 2019) as part of leadership development. The programmes were designed according to the development needs of the respective countries. The tuition fees are fully funded by Temasek Foundation, a non-profit organisation in Singapore, while respective organising agencies from the home countries will pay for the airfares, accommodation and living expenses. Table 9.1 provides an overview of the training attended by the officials from Cambodia, Thailand and Vietnam.

Table 9.1 Overview of training attended by officials from Cambodia, Thailand and Vietnam

	Cambodia	Thailand	Vietnam
Organising Home Agency/ Body	Economics and Finance Institute of the Ministry of Economy and Finance	OCSC	Monitoring Office of Programme 165 (MOP165)
Theme of Training	Public Leadership, Administration, Policy and Governance: Experiences of Singapore	High Performance and Potential System (HiPPS) Capability Development Program	'Train the Trainer' Programme in governance, public policy and administration strategies
Focus Areas	Anti-corruption, Urban Planning and Talent Management	Singapore Smart Nation Experience; Community Building; Collaborative Competency; Innovative Thinking and Internet of Things (IoT)	Governance, Urban Planning and Development, Education Policy, Economic Policy
Trainees	180 Senior leaders from different line ministries, agencies and provinces/ municipality	100 Entry to middle-level officials from HiPPS	283 Key leaders from all 63 Vietnam's provinces

From the topics that were covered in the respective training programmes, it is observed that in terms of the development stage, Cambodia is the least developed among the three countries and Thailand is the most developed. Cambodia is focusing more on urban development and capacity building while Thailand is keen to learn from Singapore's experience in public sector innovations and Smart Nation initiatives in line with the country's Thailand 4.0 strategy. For Vietnam, while emphasis is also on urban development and good governance, its stage of industrialisation is more advanced than Cambodia. As stipulated in the sponsorship from Temasek Foundation (except for Thailand which was co-funded by OCSC and NTU), each participant will train/mentor at least three other officials within 1 year, upon completion of the training. Such train-the-trainer (TTT) model focuses on initially training a person or people who, in turn, train other people at their home agency. Using the TTT model, participants who have completed the training will share their knowledge with their colleagues to build a core team of skilled administrators. There are a number of potential advantages to train-the-trainer approaches, the most obvious being to reach larger audiences through subsequent training activities led by those who were trained initially (Orfaly et al., 2005).

In addition, the trainees were also able to apply the concepts and models learned from the training in their different country contexts. For example, the second batch of participants from the Vietnam General Confederation of Labour (VGCL) reported that they started a new project to build about 1,700 blocks of affordable housing for workers which will benefit more than 8,000 workers and their families. This project was conceived and conceptualised on the basis of Singapore's experience of building public housing for the populace. Some smaller applications include implementing the paperless system within their own departments as a move towards computerisation of administrative processes.

Although there were no known established criteria in the selection of participants other than being middle- to senior-level officials from diverse domains, they could also be the ones selected for grooming and promotion. Many of the participants from Cambodia and Vietnam who have attended the EDP were promoted upon their return. For Cambodia, 13 of the participants (7.2 per cent) were promoted after completion of the programme. Out of the 13, 7 (54 per cent) were promoted to leaders at the ministry level either as Secretary (equivalent to the Head of Ministry) or under-Secretary (Deputy Head of Ministry). Four (31 per cent) were promoted as division heads (divisions are the various execution arms of the ministries), while one was promoted from central government to member of the party and another as provincial governor. For Vietnam, out of the 78 who were promoted, 42 of them (54 per cent) were promoted as directors at the subprovince department level, 15 (19 per cent) were promoted from subprovince or district leaders to provincial leaders, 10 (13 per cent) were promoted as party leaders from central government, the remaining 14 per cent (11) were promoted from below district level to the district level, provincial and party level.

As we witness the growing phenomenon of developing countries in Southeast Asia sending middle- to senior-level public officials to Singapore for leadership training, it will be more relevant to focus particularly on the contextual dimension, which calls to understand leadership as responsive and dynamic to emerging situations (Kennedy et al., 2013). Taking account of the uniqueness of Singapore's political situation and size, its experience cannot be transplanted wholesale to the participants' countries because of economic, administrative, cultural, operational and other differences; some aspects could be adopted or adapted to suit the specific needs and circumstances of their countries (Saxena, 2011).

10 Assessing talent strategies within the context of inclusive–exclusive tension paradigm

Narrow definition of talents

In Chapter 2, we have discussed that the rising theme of talent management in the public sector is with regard to the inclusive versus exclusive strategy (Dries, 2013; Gallardo-Gallardo et al., 2013; Boselie & Thunnissen, 2017; Gallardo-Gallardo & Thunnissen, 2015; Lee & Rezaei, 2019) According to Glenn (2012), an inclusive approach is more likely to occur in collective bargaining environments; therefore, formalised TM programmes that are usually exclusive are largely limited to executives and non-bargaining groups. Due to increased numbers of retirements and a labour market shortage, the public sector also shows a tendency to favour such an exclusive approach to recruiting high-calibre candidates to fill and replace the leadership pipeline (Delfgaauw & Dur, 2010; Glenn, 2012; Poocharoen & Lee, 2013). The tension arises because of the different definitions of talent; the narrow definition that pertains to certain people with special traits, intrinsic gifts, skills, knowledge, experience, intelligence, judgement, attitude, character etc. will lead to an exclusive talent strategy. On the other hand, a broader definition of talents taking regards to the ability and potential to perform, considering everyone in the organisation collectively and equally will lead to an inclusive talent strategy.

The talent schemes we have reviewed so far in the five countries are considered exclusive as they are designed to attract specific individuals that the respective public sectors want to groom as part of succession planning. This is also confirmed by the schemes for scholarship and leadership development, where only the identified few are selected through their performance, experience or stringent assessment to join the senior management or administrative service. Although talent Management schemes are an exclusive approach, from the assessment of the scholarship, executive development, leadership development schemes and performance management in the five countries, there are varying degrees along the inclusive–exclusive continuum among countries and among the levels of the scheme (Figure 10.1).

Figure 10.1 Talent schemes of Singapore, Malaysia, Thailand, Cambodia and Vietnam within the inclusive–exclusive spectrum

Overall, Cambodia's talent strategy is the most exclusive among the five countries. This is likely attributed to the limited resources and budget that the country's public sector possesses. Hence, the funding towards talent management in the public sector is dedicated to developing teachers and senior management. Singapore which used to have an exclusive approach to identifying and developing talents specifically towards certain 'best and brightest' as defined of academic excellence has in the past 5 years evolved towards a more inclusive approach that recognises the potential and performance of in-service officers to have opportunity to be groomed as specialised leaders. The next section will discuss the tension between the inclusiveness and exclusiveness of talent definitions at each level of the TM schemes by discussing the duality and ambiguity of talent in these schemes (Buttiens & Hondeghem, 2015; Meyers, 2016; Thunnissen & Buttiens, 2017).

Talent in the pre-service scholarship scheme: equity versus differentiation

On the basis of the studies of the respective TM schemes in the four Asian countries, I concur that defining talent is first and foremost in the public sector (Poocharoen & Lee, 2013; Swailes & Blackburn, 2016, Thunnissen & Buttiens, 2017). Defining and conceptualising talent is highly influenced by the factors of differentiation – in the pre-service scheme the definition is dominated by academic achievements. As suggested by Lepak and Snell (1999), differentiating groups of employees is likely to cause tension with the principle of equity. The principles of equity (equal opportunity) try to ensure that the most capable person is selected as well as the right of every individual to be given fair consideration for any job for which they are skilled and qualified. From the assessment of pre-service schemes, the preferred practice of Singapore, Malaysia and Thailand is to recruit high-school leavers through scholarships, whereas Cambodia offers scholarships to fresh graduates from elite schools to pursue PhDs. These scholarship recipients will eventually be bonded to serve in the allocated or selected organisations. Due to the scarcity of resources and budget in the public sector, the scholars will inevitably be differentiated and provided with more opportunities and exposures when they join the organisations as they are the 'best and brightest' (Neo & Chen, 2007) and expected to outperform other non-scholars. This differentiation hence leads to the tension of inequality as not all employees at the same ranking will have equal opportunities to perform.

Among the countries, Cambodia's scholarship scheme is the most exclusive. It only offers scholarships to fresh graduates to pursue PhDs in overseas elite schools. These scholars will return to serve the public service upon completion of their studies and they will be appointed in the grade A scheme.

Another scholarship scheme is only for eligible teacher-candidates from disadvantaged areas to undertake a one-year pre-service training at the National Institute of Education (NIE). Hence, both scholarship schemes offer limitations to the choice of degree (must be Ph.D.), domain (teaching) and institutions (elite schools and NIE). Although Singapore's approach to the selection of candidates is more stringent than the other three countries, assessed primarily based on their high school academic results and Co-Curricular Activities (CCA) records, there is a wide choice of studies and institutions that applicants can choose from including uniform or non-uniform, general or specialise. Besides scholarships offered and administered centrally by PSC, there are also other scholarships offered by statutory boards that promote sectoral developments, e.g., technology and social. In Malaysia, the academic criteria are not of high priority and there is also a wide range of courses with some preferred domains such as medicine and dentistry to choose from. It has also included scholarships for diplomas. However, ethnicity still forms part of the evaluation weighting. Although the intention is to achieve representativeness in the population of the community, it often invites criticism of favouritism towards the Malay community. Compared to the other three countries, Vietnam and Thailand do not confine talents based on past academic achievements, ethnicity or choice of school. However, Vietnam only offers scholarships to fresh high school leavers who are pursuing studies that are not offered in Vietnam. For Thailand, scholarships are open to all, and candidates are required to sit for standard entry examinations, therefore providing fair opportunities for all who are interested and qualified (Poocharoen & Lee, 2013). It should be noted that the Development of Science and Mathematics Talented Project (DPST) and Ministry of Science and Technology (MST) scholarship schemes are reserved for candidates who demonstrate a special flair for science and technology disciplines.

Talent in the executive development scheme: general versus specialisation

Another inclusive–exclusive talent tension is over the principle of professionalism (Noordegraaf, 2016) and it is argued that many professionals receive special treatment or have a special position within public sector organisations as they are considered to be among the most valuable workers there. Overall, the executive development schemes for in-service officers are perceived to be inclusive, as the public sector does not favour certain specialisations. Even for the relatively new Public Service Leadership Programme (PSLP) in Singapore, there are now two separate tracks namely general and sectoral. Appointment of in-service officers into PSLP is via the annual 'In-Service Nomination Exercise' as nominated by their reporting officers through assessment of their performance and potential.

Compared to the previous HiPO scheme which is less transparent, PSLP provides clear criteria and for the sectoral pathway, it had well-defined competencies based on fixed competency frameworks for each of the six sectors (Bhatta, 2001; Mau, 2009). This offers more clarity to both the officers and reporting superiors when assessing their performance and determining training needs, hence improving transparency in the scheme for high potentials. The scholarship receivers will also be automatically appointed to PSLP upon completion of their studies and joining the service. PSLP is also opened for applications from graduates with little experience and mid-career switchers to encourage talents from other sectors but rich experience to join the service. For applicants who prefer specialised career in the public sector, they can also choose the specialised pathways or join the MAP offered by different statutory boards. Those who are appointed to PSLP and wished to remain in the general path will be appointed to the AS.

The PSED in Thailand and PTD in Malaysia are all designed for officers interested in general administration, and once enrolled in the schemes, they will receive the same training, development, rewards and benefits. There is no special treatment for officers in specialised professions since the emphasis is to groom the most competent managers in the public sector (Delfgaauw & Dur, 2010; Day et al., 2014). While there is no known specific scheme for general in-service civil servants in Cambodia, there is a fast-track scheme for existing teachers with no bachelor's degree as well as special training and professional development opportunities offered to STEM teachers and administrators. In line with the vision of improving the quality of primary and secondary education, these specialised schemes are designed for the teaching profession only.

Talent in the leadership development scheme: high performers versus high potential

The high performers versus high potential tension is prevalent in the fast-track leadership development schemes that parachute high-calibre officers to senior positions (Neo & Chen, 2007; Scullion et al., 2010; CIPD, 2012). Based on the premise that officers chosen for these fast-track programmes have demonstrated higher levels of competence and performance, only a small group of selected in-service officers in the four countries (except Vietnam) are recommended. However, the operationalisation of organisational goals in relation to individual performance is complex in the public sector (Ulrich & Ulrich, 2010; Hasnain et al., 2012). Given the increasing complexity in the public sector that often leads to conflicting goals that need to satisfy a diverse group of stakeholders, it is hard to determine performance in the context of the public sector (Collings, 2014). Although TM schemes designed to attract and retain high-achieving individuals emphasise individual performance, public service and value are often achieved as a team effort and not alone (Boselie & Thunnissen, 2017). Therefore, all employees desire to be treated fairly, as determined by the rewards (monetary and non-monetary) they receive compared to others in the organisation and by how the organisation comes to the decision concerning the reward. From an employee's perspective, fair procedures may be in place but it is the practice of fairness by supervisors that demonstrates whether justice actually occurs or not.

There are two approaches to ensure fairness. One is to judge a person by his or her competencies and the other is to look at his or her actual performance. The candidates in all these four countries are nominated by their direct reporting officers and recommended by the organisations to be enrolled in the fast-track schemes. Candidates in Cambodia not only need to have adequate experience and have performed consistently, they are also required to have attained a Ph.D. before they can be enrolled into the fast-track scheme. In Malaysia, high-potential officers need to have performed very well for the past 3 years and also need to pass additional tests before admission into the fast-track scheme. Thailand takes the most inclusive approach, as the HiPPS and NWLDP only provide accelerated training and exposure with some small bonuses as an incentive but both schemes do not guarantee a promotion. In Singapore, the AS scheme is a fast-track scheme that provides milestone trainings, rotations and fixed pathways for appointed officers to move up the grades and finally achieve the final grade that was determined by their CEP scores at the beginning of their career. CEP score is based on competencies such as educational merits, intellectual and leadership qualities. Scholars are usually rated with higher CEP scores and will be exposed to high-profile projects – therefore, they are deemed to be performing better than the rest of the officers and so will be enrolled into the AS scheme (the majority of the AOs are scholars). Recognising the criticism of such a system after many years, it is decided in 2020 that it will no longer be the 'single most important determinant' of his or her career development and progression. Facing criticism of scholars being favoured to be appointed to the AS, the scheme is currently open for application to candidates (in-service and mid-career switchers) with outstanding career history, relevant working experience and a proven track record of leadership qualities.

Performance-linked incentive scheme: collective versus individual

All employees desire to be treated fairly as determined by the rewards they receive compared to others in the organisation and by how the organisation comes to the decision concerning the reward (Poocharoen & Lee, 2013). Objectives are ambiguous in the public sector and difficult to quantify and separate individual or collective achievements. Singapore is the only country among the five countries and in the region that implemented performance-linked incentives for individual officers in the public sector. While Thailand and Malaysia have some form of incentive scheme, there is no apparent linkage of performance-based incentive schemes in Cambodia and Vietnam. Singapore has implemented performance bonuses for all public-sector employees since the year 2000. To enable fair assessment, there was a clear set of criteria pre-established by PSD. However, these are generic criteria. Therefore, individual supervisors will need to meet up with individual staff at the beginning of the yearly evaluation cycle to agree upon the set of key performance indicators. There is also the individual development plan being discussed at the same time to address the training needs for the individual officers so that he/she will be sent for adequate training in fulfilment of the 100 training hours. Although Singapore has the most well-defined performance appraisal system which leads to performance-based pay and incentives, the promotion runs on a quota-based curve, of which the top performers only make up 15 per cent of the distribution, while 80 per cent will be rated as developing contributor or average, and the rest of the 5 per cent will be the poor performers (Quah, 2010b; Poocharoen & Lee, 2013). The final scoring will also be determined by the senior management and not the immediate supervisors. Due to this, officers often can 'game' the system and get involved in high exposure projects or events so that they can be recognised. Therefore, often the outcome of projects is not measured in the longer term and team effort is often not being recognised in such exclusive measurement of individual achievements. Thailand's bonus-like scheme is based on the department's performance and not individual performance. However, only the department heads and officers are awarded; the low-ranking officers who did most of the operational job were not being recognised. For Malaysia, the pay increment which is linked to the performance is only a small component of 2 per cent, and the larger component is still dependent on the grade of service which is group based.

Conclusion: towards an inclusive talent strategy for leadership succession

Competency building and talent management among public servants have become imperative, one that aims to provide competent managers to conduct government operations in the transformative management and governance context. Talent management as a field of study is evolving from its infancy to adolescence, and especially with heightened attention in the public sector. Originally, talent management has been coined as a highly exclusive construct especially in the public sector (Delfgaauw & Dur, 2010; Glenn, 2012; Poocharoen & Lee, 2013; Lee & Rezaei, 2019). It is a tool for employees who are valuable and unique (Lepak & Snell, 1999), display high potential or high performance (Silzer & Church, 2009), and/or occupy strategically important positions within the organisation (Huselid et al., 2005), especially in the context of the public sector with limited budget and resources to offer equal development opportunities to all officers. However, it is notable that inclusive talent management which is defined as 'the recognition and acceptance that all employees have talent together with the ongoing evaluation and deployment of employees in positions that give the best fit and opportunity (via participation) for employees to use those talents' (Swailes et al., 2014, p. 5) acknowledges the best in all employees and they should be allowed to realise their full potential.

There has been a significant shift from Singapore's exclusive approach to identifying and developing the 'best and brightest' primarily based on strong academic achievement to a more inclusive approach to recognising an individual's unique strengths and abilities. This indeed signifies in the war for talent whereby the public sector is not the 'preferred employer of the day' especially to attract the millennials, that the public sectors in Southeast Asia need to shift away from its bureaucratic roots inherited from the colonisation and consider talent management within the context of the current reform landscape. The context requires an increased focus on tackling inequalities, increased integration, increased collaboration, shared leadership, effective approaches to joint resourcing and community empowerment especially towards resolving immediate and challenging issues. All these will require new skills and attributes of talents they require across their organisations to deliver against the ambitions of the reform agenda and to improve the lives of the communities they serve, as well as to identify the skill gaps and how they will address these. Even as countries such as Cambodia and Vietnam which are unable to match remuneration to the private sector, efforts should be made to recognise effort and reward in none-monetary terms to motivate good works and curb corruption.

The COVID-19 pandemic that has crippled the whole world is one good reminder that a responsive government that has a diverse pool of talents is critical to quickly come out with policies and initiatives to contain the pandemic and revive the affected social and economic aspects (Liu et al., 2020). Singapore was a successful example that managed to contain the pandemic and revive its ailing economy after a short setback that led to partial lockdown for about 2 months. Its rapid and progressive responses in accordance with the fast-evolving situation were achieved through a coordinated Whole-of-government approach and a cocktail of digital solutions that augment the government's efforts (Lee, 2020).

As the country matures, the aspirations of its citizens will evolve to contend with the rapidly changing global environment. The repercussions of globalisation have led the public sectors globally to rethink their strategies and visions. The new millennium marks a new era, in which the employment landscape is filled with the new generation that has gradually shifted from academic pursuers to employees, and, eventually, main players of the job market. This will require public services to focus on more inclusive talent management approaches and leadership development at all levels across their organisations, not just on specific individuals or groups. Given the increasing emphasis on community empowerment, it will be vital that those working in the frontline are developed, supported and empowered to work in different ways to support individuals and communities that they are serving. It will also require public services to work with and resource individuals and communities to develop and contribute their capacity and talents to achieving better outcomes. All these post-NPM approaches to governance and delivery of public services entail more group effort and cooperation; therefore, as countries in the region are considering implementing performance-linked remuneration system, it should be designed to reward groups' and departments' efforts.

References

Abas, A. (2019). 1.71 Million Civil Servants on Govt Payroll as of March 2019. New Straits Times. Retrieved on August 31, 2020, from https://www.nst.com.my/news/government-public-policy/2019/04/484308/171-million-civil-servants-govt-payroll-march-2019

Adetunji, J. (2012, June 29). Civil service training strategy cuts 'massive duplication'. *The Guardian*. Retrieved from www.theguardian.com/public-leaders-network/blog/2012/jun/29/central-government-civil-service

Ananthan, S. S., Manaf, H. A., Hidayati, M., & Dewi, D. S. K. (2019). The development of talent management in Malaysian public sector: A comprehensive review. *Problems and Perspectives in Management, 17*(2), 242–253.

Anderson, B. R. O'G. (1991). *Imagined communities: Reflections on the origin and spread of nationalism.* London: Verso.

Armstrong, M. (2007). *A handbook of human resource management practice.* London: Kogan Page.

ASEAN. (2017). *Complementarities between the ASEAN community vision 2025 and the United Nations 2030 agenda for sustainable development: A framework for action* (Rep.). Thailand: United Nations Economic and Social Commission for Asia and the Pacific (ESCAP).

Asian Development Bank (ADB). (2016). *Kingdom of Cambodia: Upper Secondary Education Sector Development Program.* Cambodia: Asian Development Bank.

Barcham, M. (2003). South-south policy transfer: The case of the Vanuatu Ombudsman's office. *Pacific Economic Bulletin, 18*(2).

Baum, A. (2020). *Vietnam's development success story and the unfinished SDG agenda.* (IMF Working Paper, Working paper No. 20/31). International Monetary Fund.

Beh, L.-S. (2018). Leadership and public sector reform in Malaysia. In E. Berman & E. Prasojo (Eds.), *Leadership and public sector reform in Asia* (Vol. 30, Public policy and governance, pp. 207–230). Bingley, UK: Emerald Publishing Limited.

Beh, L.-S., & Kennan, W. R. (2013). Leadership in the East: A social capital perspective. In J. Rajasekar & L.-S. Beh (Eds.), *Culture and gender in leadership.* London: Palgrave Macmillan.

Bennett, C. (1991). What is policy convergence and what causes it? *British Journal of Political Science, 21*, 215–233.

Benson, D., & Jordan, A. (2011). What Have We Learned from Policy Transfer Research? Dolowitz and Marsh Revisited. *Political Studies Review, 9*(3), 366–378.

Berger, L., & Berger, D. (2010). *The talent management handbook, second edition: Creating a sustainable competitive advantage by selecting, developing, and promoting the best people*. New York: McGraw-Hill.

Berman, E., Bowman, J., West, J., & Van Wart, M. (2009). *Human resource management in public service: Paradoxes, processes and problems*. Thousand Oaks, CA: SAGE.

Bhatnagar, J. (2007). Talent management strategy of employee engagement in Indian ITES employees: Key to retention. *Employee Relations, 29*(6), 640–663.

Bhatta, G. (2001). Enabling the cream to rise to the top: A cross-jurisdictional comparison of competencies for senior managers in the public sector. *Public Performance and Management, 25*(2), 194–207.

Björkman, I., Ehrnrooth, M., Mäkelä, K., Smale, A., & Sumelius, J. (2013). Talent or not? Employee reactions to talent identification. *Human Resource Management, 52*(2), 195–214.

Blunt, P., & Turner, M. (2005). Decentralisation, democracy and development in a post-conflict society: Commune councils in Cambodia. *Public Administration and Development, 25*(1), 75–87. doi:10.1002/pad.349

Borgonovi, E., Anessi-Pessina, E., & Bianchi, C. (Eds.). (2018). *Outcome-based performance management in the public sector* (Vol. 2, System dynamics for performance management). Cham, Switzerland: Springer.

Boselie, P., & Thunnissen, M. (2017). Talent management in the public sector: Managing tensions and dualities. In D. G. Collings, K. Mellahi, & W. F. Cascio (Eds.), *The Oxford handbook of talent management* (pp. 420–439). Oxford: Oxford University Press.

Broome, A., & Seabrooke, L. (2015). Shaping policy curves: Cognitive authority in transnational capacity building. *Public Administration, 93*(4), 956–972.

Buttiens, D., & Hondeghem, A. (2015). Strategic choices regarding talent management in the Flemish public sector. *Society and Economy, 37*(1), 49–72.

Cappelli, P. (2008). *Talent on demand: Managing talent in an age of uncertainty*. Boston, MA: Harvard Business School Press.

Chambers, E. G., Foulon, M., Handfield-Jones, H., Hankin, S. M., & Michaels, E. G., III. (1998). The war for talent. *The McKinsey Quarterly, 1*(3), 44–57.

Chan, C. S. (2020). Changes to civil service's currently estimated potential system to kick in progressively from 2021. *Today Online*. Retrieved January 15, 2021, from www.todayonline.com/singapore/changes-civil-services-currently-estimated-potential-system-kick-progressively-2021-chan

Chandler, D. P. (1986). The Kingdom of Kampuchea, March–October 1945: Japanese-sponsored independence in Cambodia in World War II. *Journal of Southeast Asian Studies, 17*(1), 80–93.

Chartered Institute for Personnel and Development (CIPD). (2012). *Resourcing and talent planning: Annual survey report*. London: Chartered Institute of Personnel and Development.

Chartered Institute for Personnel and Development (CIPD). (2016). The future of talent in Singapore. Retrieved March 19, 2019, from www.cipd. asia/knowledge/reports/future-talent-singapore

Chin, J. (2011). Chapter 7: History and context of public administration in Malaysia. In E. M. Berman (Ed.), *Public administration in Southeast Asia: Thailand, Philippines, Malaysia, Hong Kong, and Macao* (1st ed., pp. 141–153). New York: Routledge.

Chua, B. H. (2008). Southeast Asia in postcolonial studies: An introduction. *Postcolonial Studies, 11*(3), 231–240.

Civil Service College. (2020). Who we are. Retrieved January 15, 2021, from www.csc.gov.sg/who-we-are

Clarke, R. (1999). Institutions for training overseas administrators: The University of Manchester's contribution. *Public Administration and Development, 19*, 521–533.

Clarke, M., & T. Scurry (2017). The Role of the Psychological Contract in Shaping Graduate Experiences: A Study of Public Sector Talent Management Programmes in the UK and Australia. *The International Journal of Human Resource Management, 29*(13), 2054–2079.

Collings, D. G. (2014). Toward mature talent management: Beyond shareholder value. *Human Resource Development Quarterly, 25*, 301–319.

Common, R. (2012). From London to Beijing: Training and development as an agent of policy learning in public management. *International Journal of Public Administration, 35*(10), 677–683.

Cornerstone. (2009). For Government: Leadership and New Technology can Solve Chronic Talent Management Illnesses. Retrieved on March 2020, from https://www.cornerstoneondemand.com/sites/default/files/whitepaper/csod-wp_knld-eng-rx-gov_2009.pdf

Cuong, T. V. (2019). Training and retraining civil servants of home affairs in Vietnam in response to the requirements of international integration. *International Journal of Human Resource Studies, 9*(1), 126–135.

Dalayga, B. (2020). Public sector must prioritise talent. *New Straits Times*. Retrieved December 1, 2020, from www.nst.com.my/opinion/letters/2020/09/622038/public-sector-must-prioritise-talent

Dana, L.P. (2014). *Asian Models of Entrepreneurship – From the Indian Union and Nepal to the Japanese Archipelago: Context, Policy and Practice*, 2nd ed., Singapore & London: World Scientific.

Davies, B., & Davies, B. J. (2010). Talent management in academics. *International Journal of Educational Management, 24*(5), 418–426.

Day, M., Shickle, D., Smith, K., & Zakariasen, K. (2014). Training public health superheroes: Five talents for public sector health leadership. *Journal of Public Health, 36*(4), 552–561.

Delfgaauw, J., & Dur, R. (2010). Managerial talent, motivation, and self-selection into public management. *Journal of Public Economics, 94*(9–10), 654–660.

Dolowitz, D. P., & Marsh, D. (2000). Learning from abroad: The role of policy transfer in contemporary policy making. *Governance, 13*(1), 5–23.

Dolowitz, D. P., & Marsh, C. (2012). The future of policy transfer research. *Political Studies, 10*, 339–345.

Downie, S., & Kingsbury, D. (2001). Political development and the re-emergence of civil society in Cambodia. *Contemporary Southeast Asia, 23*(1), 43–64. doi:10.1355/cs23-1c

Drezner, D. W. (2001). Globalization and policy convergence. *The International Studies Review, 3*, 53–78.

Dries, N. (2013). The psychology of talent management: A review and research agenda. *Human Resource Management Journal, 23*(4), 272–285.

Duan, Y., Nie, W. Y., & Coakes, E. (2006). Identifying key factors affecting transnational knowledge transfer. *Information and Management, 47*, 356–363.

Duggett, M. (2001). Cross-channel perspectives on British civil service training. *Public Policy and Administration, 16*(4), 96–105.

Economic Planning Unit (EPU). (2016). Government Delivery Transforming the civil service to productivity (Chapter 9). In Eleventh Malaysia Plan 2016–2020. Kuala Lumpur: Percetakan Nasional Malaysia Berhad.

Eden, D. (1984). Self-fulfilling prophecy as a management tool: Harnessing Pygmalion. *Academy of Management Review, 9*(1), 64–73.

Encyclopædia Britannica. (2019). World War II and its aftermath. Retrieved October 23, 2020, from www.britannica.com/place/Cambodia/World-War-II-and-its-aftermath

Enterprise Singapore. (2021). Management associate programme. Retrieved January 15, 2021, from www.enterprisesg.gov.sg/Careers/Management-Associate-Programme

Evans, M. (2009). Policy transfer in critical perspective. *Policy Studies, 30*(3), 243–268.

Evans, M. (2017). *Policy transfer in global perspective*. London: Routledge.

Ezra, F. V. (1979). *Japan as number one: Lessons for America*. Cambridge: Harvard University Press.

Fernando, J. M. (2019). A playmaker and moderator: Lord Reid and the framing of the Malayan federal constitution. *Journal of Southeast Asian Studies, 50*(3), 431–449.

Fernando, J. M., & Rajagopal, S. (2017). Fundamental liberties in the Malayan constitution and the search for a balance, 1956–1957. *International Journal of Asia Pacific Studies, 13*(1), 1–28. doi:10.21315/ijaps2017.13.1.1

Frank, F., & Taylor, C. (2004). Talent management trends that will shape the future. *Human Resource Planning, 27*(1), 33–41.

Gallardo-Gallardo, E., Dries, N., & Gonzàlez-Cruz, T. (2013). What is the meaning of 'talent' in the world of work? *Human Resource Management Review, 23*(4), 290–300.

Gallardo-Gallardo, E., & Thunnissen, M. (2015). Standing on the shoulders of giants? A critical review of empirical talent management research. *Employee Relations, 38*(1), 31–56. doi:10.1108/ER-10-2015-0194

Garrow, V., & Hirsh, W. (2008). Talent management: Issues of focus and fit. *Public Personnel Management, 37*(4), 389–402.

GCPSE. (2015). *UNDP and the making of Singapore's public service: Lessons from Albert Winsemius*. Singapore: Global Centre for Public Service Excellence.

Gellner, E. (1983). *Nations and nationalism*. Ithaca: Cornell University Press.

Glenn, T. (2012). The state of talent management in Canada's public sector. *Canadian Public Administration, 55*(1), 25–51.

Gopinathan, S. (2012). *Education and the nation state: The selected works of S. Gopinathan* (World library of educationalists series). London: Routledge. doi:10.4324/9780203078815

The Government of Vietnam. (2017a). *Nghị định số 34/2017/NĐ-CP ngày 3/4/2017 quy định chức năng, nhiệm vụ, quyền hạn và cơ cấu tổ chức của Bộ Nội vụ (Decree No. 34/2017/ NĐ-CP dated 3/4/2017 defining the functions, tasks, powers and organisational structure of the Ministry of Home Affairs).* Hanoi: The Government of Vietnam.

The Government of Vietnam. (2017b). *Nghị định số 101/2017/NĐ-CP ngày 01/9/2017 của Chính phủ về đào tạo, bồi dưỡng cán bộ, công chức, viên chức (Decree No. 101/2017/NĐ-CP dated 1/9/2017 on the training and retraining of officials and civil servants).* Hanoi: The Government of Vietnam.

Groves, K. (2011). Talent management best practices: How exemplary health care organizations create value in a down economy. *Health Care Management Review, 36*(3), 227–240.

Guo, Y., & Phua, C. (2014). *Our Singapore conversation: Bridging the great divide (case study)*. Singapore: Lee Kuan Yew School of Public Policy, National University of Singapore.

Gupta, P. P., Dirsmith, M. W., & Fogarty, T. J. (1994). Coordination and control in a government agency: Contingency and institutional theory perspectives on GAO audits. *Administrative Science Quarterly, 39*, 264–284.

Haque, M. S. (1996). The contextless nature of public administration in third world countries. *International Review of Administrative Sciences, 62*(3), 315–329.

Haque, M. S. (2004). Governance and bureaucracy in Singapore: Contemporary reforms and implications. *International Political Science Review, 25*(2), 227–240.

Haque, M. S. (2006). Reforming public administration in Southeast Asia: Trends and impacts. *Public Organization Review, 4*, 361–371.

Haque, M. S. (2007). Theory and practice of public administration in Southeast Asia: Traditions, directions, and impacts. *International Journal of Public Administration, 30*(12–14), 1297–1326. doi:10.1080/01900690701229434

Harris, L., & Foster, C. (2010). Aligning talent management with approaches to equality and diversity. *Equality, Diversity and Inclusion: An International Journal, 29*(5), 422–435.

Hasnain, Z., Manning, N., & Pierskalla, J. (2012). *Performance-related pay in the public sector: A review of theory and evidence* (Policy Research Working Paper, Working paper No. 6043). Washington, DC: World Bank.

Hausman, D. (2010). *Policy leaps and implementation obstacles: Civil service reform in Vietnam, 1998–2009.* Princeton, NJ: Trustees of Princeton University for Successful Societies, Princeton University.

Hays Specialist Recruitment Ltd. (2012). *The changing face of the public sector: How employers need to adapt.* United Kingdom: Hays.

Heinrich, C. (2002). Outcomes-based performance management in the public sector: Implications for government accountability and effectiveness. *Public Administration Review, 62*(6), 712–725.

Henderson, J. (2012). Planning for success: Singapore, the model city-state? *Journal of International Affairs, 65*(2), 69–83.

Hofstede, G. (1981). Management control of public and not-for-profit activities. *Accounting, Organizations and Society, 6,* 193–211.

Holzinger, K., & Knill, C. (2005). Causes and Conditions of Cross-national Policy convergence. *Journal of European Public Policy, 12*(5), 775–796.

Hood, C. (1991). A public management for all seasons? *Public Administration, 69*(1), 3–19.

Hood, C., & Peters, G. (2004). The middle aging of new public management: Into the age of paradox? *Journal of Public Administration Research and Theory, 14*(3), 267–282.

Huque, A. S., & Jongruck, P. (2020). Civil service reforms in Hong Kong and Thailand: Similar goals, different paths. *Public Administration and Policy: An Asia-Pacific Journal, 23*(2), 111–123.

Huselid, M., Beatty, R., & Becker, B. (2005). A players or a positions? The strategic logic of workforce management. *Harvard Business Review, 83,* 110–117, 154.

Ingham, J. (2006). Closing the talent management gap: Harnessing your employees' talent to deliver optimum business performance. *Strategic HR Review, 5*(3), 20–23.

Jessop, B., & Sum, N.-L. (2000). An entrepreneurial city in action: Hong Kong's emerging strategies in and for (inter) urban competition. *Urban Studies, 37*(12), 2287–2313.

Johnsen, Å. (2005). What does 25 years of experience tell us about the state of performance measurement in public policy and management? *Public Money and Management, 25*(1), 9–17.

Jones, D. S. (2016). Governance and meritocracy: A study of policy implementation in Singapore. In J. S. T. Quah (Ed.), *The role of the public bureaucracy in policy implementation in five ASEAN countries* (pp. 297–369). Cambridge: Cambridge University Press.

Jones, D. S. (2018). Leadership and public sector reform in Singapore. In E. Berman & E. Prasojo (Eds.), *Leadership and public sector reform in Asia* (Vol. 30, Public policy and governance, pp. 179–205). Bingley, UK: Emerald Publishing Limited.

JPA. (2021). Profile of PSD. Retrieved January 3, 2021, from www.jpa.gov. my/info-korporat/profil-jpa

Kelly, M., Yutthaphonphinit, P., Seubsman, S. A., & Sleigh, A. (2012). Development policy in Thailand: From top-down to grass roots. *Asian Social Science, 8*(13), 29–39.

116   *References*

Kennedy, F., Carroll, B., & Francoeur, J. (2013). Mindset not skill set evaluating in new paradigms of leadership development. *Advances in Developing Human Resources, 15*, 10–26.

Khmer Times. (2017). Slash Civil Servant Recruiting: Hun Sen. Phnom Penh, Cambodia, 23 August 2017.

Khuong, V. (2015). Can Vietnam achieve more robust economic growth? Insights from a comparative analysis of economic reforms in Vietnam and China. *Journal of Southeast Asian Economies, 32*(1), 52–83.

Kim, C., & Scullion, H. (2011). Exploring the links between corporate social responsibility and global talent management: A comparative study of the UK and Korea. *European Journal of International Management, 5*, 501–523.

Kim, P. S. (2008). How to attract and retain the best in government. *International Review of Administrative Sciences, 74*(4), 637–652.

Klievink, B., & Janssen, M. (2009). Realizing joined-up government: Dynamic capabilities and stage models for transformation. *Government Information Quarterly, 26*, 275–284.

Knill, C. (2005). Introduction: Cross-national policy convergence: Concepts, approaches and explanatory factors. *Journal of European Public Policy, 12*(5), 764–774.

Korm, R. (2011). *The relationship between pay and performance in the Cambodian civil service* (Doctorate thesis, University of Canberra, 2011). Canberra: University of Canberra.

Kratoska, P. H., & Goto, K. (2015). Chapter 21: Japanese occupation of Southeast Asia, 1941–1945. In R. J. Bosworth & J. A. Maiolo (Eds.), *The Cambridge history of the Second World War* (Vol. 2, pp. 533–557). Cambridge, United Kingdom: Cambridge University Press.

Kravariti, F., & Johnston, K. (2020). Talent management: A critical literature review and research agenda for public sector human resource management. *Public Management Review, 22*(1), 75–95.

Kumar, J. A., & Ganesh, L. S. (2009). Research on knowledge transfer in organizations: A morphology. *Journal of Knowledge Management, 13*(4), 161–174.

Lee, C. (2018). The leadership of balancing control and autonomy in public sector networks: The case of Singapore. *Journal of Asian Public Policy, 11*(2), 151–172.

Lee, C. (2020). Responses of Singapore to COVID-19 Pandemic: The Whole-of-Government Approach. In Paul Joyce, Fabienne Maron, & Purshottama Sivanarain Reddy, (Eds.), *Good Public Governance in a Global Pandemic*. Brussels: IIAS-IISA.

Lee, C., Ma, L., & Zhou, Y. S. (2017). The changing dynamics of policy experiment in Singapore: Does the 2011 general election make a difference? *Asian Journal of Political Science, 25*(3), 287–306.

Lee, C., & Rezaei, S. (2019). Talent management strategies in the public sector: A review of talent management schemes in Southeast Asia. In Y. Liu (Ed.), *Research handbook of international talent management*. Cheltenham: Edward Elgar Publishing.

Lee, H.L. (2015). Choice and Conviction: The Foreign Policy of a Little Red Dot. 2015 S Rajaratnam Lecture by Prime Minister Lee Hsien Loong, 27 November 2015.

Lee, J. C. H. (2018). Outrage in Malaysia: The politics of taking offence. *East Asia*, *35*, 249–265.

Legrand, T., & McConnell, A. (2012). *Emergency policy*. Farnham: Ashgate.

Lepak, D., & Snell, S. (1999). The human resource architecture: Toward a theory of human capital allocation and development. *Academy of Management Review*, *24*, 31–48.

Lewis, R., & Heckman, R. (2006). Talent management: Critical review. *Human Resource Management Review*, *16*(2), 139–154.

Lim, D., & Morris, M. (2006). Influence of trainee characteristics, instructional satisfaction, and organizational climate on perceived learning and training transfer. *Human Resource Development Quarterly*, *17*, 85–115.

Lim, H. (2007). Ethnic representation in the Malaysian bureaucracy: The development and effects of Malay domination. *International Journal of Public Administration*, *30*(12–14), 1503–1524. doi:10.1080/01900690701229731

Liu, H., & Wang, T. Y. (2018). China and the 'Singapore model': Perspectives from mid-level cadres and implications for transnational knowledge transfer. *The China Quarterly*, 1–24.

Liu, Y., Lee, J. M., & Lee, C. (2020). The challenges and opportunities of a global health crisis: The management and business implications of COVID-19 from an Asian perspective. *Asian Business & Management*, *19*, 277–297. doi:https://doi.org/10.1057/s41291-020-00119-x

Low, J. (2016). Chapter 9: Milestone programs for the administrative service in the Singapore public service. In A. S. Podger & J. Wanna (Eds.), *Sharpening the sword of state: Building executive capacities in the public services of the Asia-Pacific* (pp. 181–212). Acton, A.C.T., Australia: Australian National University Press.

Low, J. (2018). Chapter 1: Neglect? The origins of Singapore's administration and administrative training prior to self-government (1819–1959). In *Inception point: The use of learning and development to reform the Singapore public service* (pp. 1–27). Singapore: World Scientific Publishing.

Macfarlane, F., Duberley, J., Fewtrell, C., & Powell, M. (2012). Talent management for NHS managers: Human resource or resourceful humans? *Public Money and Management*, *32*(6), 445–452.

Mahbubani, K. (2018). *Has the West lost it?* London: Penguin.

Majeed, R. (2010). *Strengthening public administration: Brazil, 1995–1998.* Princeton, NJ: Innovations for Successful Societies.

Malaysian Digest. (2017). M'sia has the highest civil service workforce in the world, is this a misconception? Retrieved December 1, 2020, from www.malaysiandigest.com/frontpage/282-main-tile/657488-malaysia-s-bloated-civilservice-we-ask-stakeholdershow-to-justify-the-numbers.htm

Manaf, N. (2010). Civil service system in Malaysia. In E. Berman (Ed.), *Public administration in Southeast Asia: Thailand, Philippines, Malaysia, Hong Kong and Macao*. Boca Raton, FL: CRC Press.

Margolin, J.-L. (2016). Connecting through colonisation? In S. Lee, *Connectivity: Facts and perspectives, II* (pp. 297–314). Singapore: Asia-Europe Foundation (ASEF).

Mau, T. (2009). Is public sector leadership distinct? A comparative analysis of core competencies in the senior executive service. In J. A. Raffel, P. Leisink, & A. E. Middlebrooks (Eds.), *Public sector leadership: International challenges and perspectives* (pp. 313–339). Cheltenham, UK and Northampton, MA, USA: Edward Elgar Publishing.

McCall, M. W., Jr. (1998). *High flyers: Developing the next generation of leaders.* Boston, MA: Harvard Business Press.

McNulty, Y., & Kaveri, G. (2019). Macro talent management in Singapore: An analysis based on local media. In V. Vaiman, P. Sparrow, R. Schuler, & D. G. Collings (Eds.), *Macro talent management in emerging and emergent markets: A global perspective.* London: Routledge.

Merchant, K. A. (1998). *Modern management control systems.* Englewood Cliffs, NJ: Prentice-Hall.

Merchant, K., & Van der Stede, W. (2003). *Management control systems: Performance measurement, evaluation and incentives.* Harlow, UK: Prentice Hall.

Meyers, M. (2016). Talent management: Towards a more inclusive understanding. *Tijdschrift voor HRM, 12,* 1–12.

Meyers, M. C., Van Woerkom, M., & Dries, N. (2013). Talent: Innate or acquired? Theoretical considerations and their implications for talent management. *Human Resource Management Review, 23*(4), 305–321.

Meyer-Sahling, J. (2011). The durability of EU civil service policy in Central and Eastern Europe after accession. *Governance: An International Journal of Policy, Administration, and Institutions, 24*(2), 231–260.

Michaels, E., Handfield-Jones, H., & Axelrod, B. (2001). *The war for talent.* Boston, MA: Harvard Business School Press.

Modell, S. (2000). Integrating management control and human resource management in public health care: Swedish case study evidence. *Financial Accountability and Management, 16*(1), 33–53.

MoEYS Ministry of Education, Youth and Sports. (2015). Mid-term review report in 2016. Retrieved from www.globalpartnership.org/sites/default/files/2016-11-cambodia-mid-term-review-education-sector-plan.pdf

Mol, N. P. (1996). Performance indicators in the Dutch department of defence. *Financial Accountability & Management, 12*(1), 71–81.

Movius, H., & Susskind, L. (2009). *Built to win: Creating a world class negotiating organization.* Boston, MA: Harvard Business School Publishing.

Mukherjee, H., Singh, J. S., Fernandez-Chung, R. M., & Marimuthu, T. (2017). Access and equity issues in Malaysian higher education. In S. Malakolunthu & N. Rengasamy (Eds.), *Policy discourses in Malaysian education* (p. 63). London: Routledge.

Nakrošis, V. (2014). Theory-based evaluation of capacity-building interventions. *Evaluation, 20*(1), 134–150.

National Education for All (EFA) Action Plan 2003–2015. (2003). No: 872/CP-KG. Hanoi.

National Library Board. (2013, September 12). Public Service Commission. Retrieved October 15, 2020, from https://eresources.nlb.gov.sg/infopedia/articles/SIP_2013-09-13_165703.html

Neo, B., & Chen, G. (2007). *Dynamic governance: Embedding culture, capabilities and change in Singapore.* Singapore: World Scientific Press.

Newberry, S., & Pallot, J. (2004). Freedom or coercion? NPM incentives in New Zealand central government departments. *Management Accounting Research, 15,* 247–266.

Newcomer, K., Allen, H., & El Baradei, L. (2010). Improving public service educational programs through assessing the performance of MPA alumni. *International Journal of Public Administration, 33*(6), 311–324.

Ngiam, T. D., & Tay, S. (2006). *A Mandarin and the making of public policy: Reflections by Ngiam Tong Dow.* Singapore: NUS Press.

Nguyen, T. A. (2006). Fiscal risks from the perspective of state-owned enterprises in Vietnam. In *Paper under sponsorship of Ministry of Finance of Vietnam.* Presented at APEC Finance Ministers' Meeting, Hanoi.

Nguyen, X. T., & Panganiban, E. M. (2000). The political dimension of local governance. In *East and Southeast Asia network for better local governments: New public management: Local political and administrative reforms.* Pasay City, Philippines: Local Government Development Foundation.

Nijs, S., Gallardo-Gallardo, E., Dries, N., & Sels, L. (2014). A multidisciplinary review into the definition, operationalization, and measurement of talent. *Journal of World Business, 49*(2), 180–191.

Noordegraaf, M. (2016). *Public management: Performance, professionalism and politics.* Basingstoke: Palgrave Macmillan.

Office of the Civil Service Commission. (1993). *King Prajadhipok and the civil service system.* Bangkok: Office of Civil Service Commission.

Office of the Civil Service Commission. (2009a). *The civil Service System of the Future: Characteristics of Civil Servants for the next Decade.* Bangkok: Office of the Civil Service Commission.

Office of the Civil Service Commission. (2009b). *Analysis of Civil Service Manpower.* Bangkok: Office of the Civil Service Commission.

Office of the Civil Service Commission. (2021). About OCSC. Retrieved January 10, 2021, from www.ocsc.go.th/english/ocsc

Ojo, A., Janowski, T., & Estevez, E. (2011). Whole-of-government approach to information technology strategy management: Building a sustainable collaborative technology environment in government. *Information Polity, 16*(3), 243–260.

Orfaly, R. A., Frances, J. C., Campbell, P., Whittemore, B., Joly, B., & Koh, H. (2005). Train-the-trainer as an educational model in public health preparedness. *Journal of Public Health Management and Practice, 11*(6), S123–S127.

Organization for Economic Co-operation and Development (OECD). (2017). *OECD public governance review: Skills for a high performing civil service.* Paris: OECD Publishing.

Organization for Economic Co-operation and Development (OECD). (2019). *Southeast Asia going digital: Connecting SMEs.* Paris: OECD Publishing. Retrieved from www.oecd.org/going-digital/southeast-asia-connecting-SMEs.pdf

Osborne, M. (2000). *Southeast Asia: An introductory history* (8th ed.). Sydney: George Allen & Unwin.

Ouchi, W. G. (1979). A conceptual framework for the design of organizational control mechanisms. *Management Science, 25*(9), 833–848.

Ouchi, W. G. (1980). Markets, bureaucracies and clans. *Administrative Science Quarterly, 25*(1), 129–141.

Painter, M. (2004). The politics of administrative reform in East and Southeast Asia: From gridlock to continuous self-improvement? *Governance, 17*(3), 361–386.

Parandekar, Suhas D., & Elisabeth K. Sedmik. (2016). "Unraveling a Secret – Vietnam's Outstanding Performance on the PISA Test." World Bank Group, policy Research Working Paper 7630.

Parliament of Singapore. (2020, February 3). System of government. Retrieved from www.parliament.gov.sg/about-us/structure/system-of-government

Peterson, C., & Seligman, M. E. P. (2004). *Character strengths and virtues: A handbook and classification*. New York, NY: Oxford University Press.

Pham, H. N. (2018). Leadership and public sector reform in Vietnam. In E. Berman & E. Prasojo (Eds.), *Leadership and public sector reform in Asia* (Vol. 30, pp. 127–149). Bingley, UK: Emerald Group Publishing.

Pike, J. E. (2012, June 02). 1863–1953: French colonial rule. Retrieved October 22, 2020, from www.globalsecurity.org/military/world/cambodia/history-france.htm

Pollitt, C. (2006). Performance management in practice: A comparative study of executive agencies. *Journal of Public Administration Research and Theory, 16*(1), 25–44.

Pollitt, C. (2009). Bureaucracies remember, post-bureaucratic organizations forget? *Public Administration, 87*(2), 198–218.

Pollitt, C., & Bouckaert, G. (2004). *Public management reform: A comparative analysis*. Oxford: Oxford University Press.

Poocharoen, O. O., & Lee, C. (2013). Talent management in the public sector: A comparative study of Singapore, Malaysia, and Thailand. *Public Personnel Review, 15*(8), 1185–1207.

Powell, M., Durose, J., Duberley, J., Exworthy, M., Fewtrell, C., MacFarlane, F., & Moss, P. (2012). *Talent management in the NHS managerial workforce: Final report*. London: National Institute for Health Research.

Project 165. (2008). Code 165-TB/TW, on 27 Jun 2008

Prum, V. (2005). Reforming Cambodian local administration: Is institutional history unreceptive for decentralization? *Forum of International Development Studies, 30*, 97–121. doi:10.18999/FORIDS.30.97

Public Service Commission. (2019). What the PSC does. Retrieved October 22, 2020, from www.psc.gov.sg/who-we-are/what-the-psc-does

Public Service Division. (2019). Building a public service ready for the future. Retrieved October 15, 2020, from www.psd.gov.sg/heartofpublicservice/our-institutions/building-a-public-service-ready-for-the-future/

Public Service Division. (2020). Our organisational structure. Retrieved October 22, 2020, from www.psd.gov.sg/who-we-are/our-organisational-structure

Public Services Commission of Malaysia. (2020). Establishment history. Retrieved October 19, 2020, from www.spa.gov.my/spa/en/psc-info/establishment-history

Putra Nurwan, S. B., & Hizatul, H. H. (2004). Model kompetensi perkhidmatan awam Malaysia. *Jurnal Pengurusan Awam, 2*(1), 79–96.

Pynes, J. (2009). *Human resource management in public and nonprofit organizations.* San Francisco, CA: Jossey-Bass.

Quah, J. S. T. (1996). Transforming the Singapore civil service for national development. In H. K. Asmerom & E. P. Reis (Eds.), *Democratization and bureaucratic neutrality* (pp. 294–312). Basingstoke: Macmillan Press.

Quah, J. S. T. (2010a). Chapter 6: Compensation: Paying for the 'best and brightest'. In *Public administration Singapore-style* (pp. 97–125). Bingley, United Kingdom: Emerald Group Publishing.

Quah, J. S. T. (Ed.). (2010b). *Public administration Singapore-style* (Vol. 19, Research in public policy analysis and management). Bingley, UK: Emerald Group Publishing.

Quah, J. S. T. (2010c). Chapter 7: Administrative reform. In *Public administration Singapore-style* (pp. 127–146). Bingley, United Kingdom: Emerald Group Publishing.

Quah, J. S. T. (2013). Curbing corruption and enhancing trust in government: Some lessons from Singapore and Hong Kong. In J. Liu, B. Hebenton, & S. Jou (Eds.), *Handbook of Asian criminology.* New York, NY: Springer.

Quah, J. S. T. (2018). Why Singapore works: Five secrets of Singapore's success. *Public Administration and Policy: An Asia-Pacific Journal, 21*(1), 5–21.

Quinlan, D., Swain, N., & Vella-Brodrick, D. A. (2012). Character strengths interventions: Building on what we know for improved outcomes. *Journal of Happiness Studies: An Interdisciplinary Forum on Subjective Well-Being, 13*(6), 1145–1163.

Radnor, Z. J., & Barnes, D. (2007). Historical analysis of performance measurement and management in operations management. *International Journal of Productivity and Performance Management, 56*(5–6), 384–396.

Reilly, P. (2008). Identifying the right course for talent management. *Public Personnel Management, 37*(4), 381–388. doi:10.1177/009102600803700401

Renushara. (2020). Budget 2021: Government introduces MyStep, providing 50,000 short-term job opportunities. Retrieved January 3, 2021, from https://worldofbuzz.com/budget-2021-government-introduces-mystep-providing-50000-short-term-job-opportunities/

Rondineli, D. (2004). *Reinventing government: The imperatives of innovation and quality.* US Small Business Administration.

Robinson, M. (2015). *From old public administration to the new public service: Implications for public sector reform in developing countries* (pp. 1–20, Rep.). Singapore: UNDP Global Centre for Public Service Excellence.

Sagarika, D., Chansukreeb, P., Choc, W., & Berman, E. (2018). E-government 4.0 in Thailand: The role of central agencies. *Information Polity, 23,* 343–353.

Samaratunge, R., Alam, Q., & Teicher, J. (2008). The new public management reforms in Asia: A comparison of South and Southeast Asian countries. *International Review of Administrative Sciences, 74*(1), 25–46. doi:10.1177/0020852307085732

Saxena, N. C. (2011). *Virtuous cycles: The Singapore public service and national development.* Singapore: United Nations Development Programme.

Schwarzer, D. (2017). Europe, the end of the West and global power shifts. *GlobalPolicy, 8*(54), 18–26.

Scullion, H., Collings, D., & Caligiuri, P. (2010). Global talent management. *Journal of World Business, 45*(2), 105–108.

Seah, C. M. (1971). *Bureaucratic evolution and political change in an emerging nation: A case study of Singapore* (Doctoral dissertation, University of Manchester, 1971). Ann Arbor, MI: ProQuest Dissertations Publishing.

Seidle, B., Fernandez, S., & Perry, J. L. (2016). Do leadership training and development make a difference in the public sector? A panel study. *Public Administration Review, 76*(4), 603–613.

Seligman, M. E. P., & Csikszentmihalyi, M. (2000). Positive psychology: An introduction. *American Psychologist, 55,* 5–14.

Sen, H. (2004, July). The rectangular strategy for growth, employment, equity and efficiency in Cambodia. Retrieved October 23, 2020, from https://policy.asiapacificenergy.org/sites/default/files/RGC_Rectangular_Strategy_2004.pdf

Sen, H. (2008, September 26). 'Rectangular strategy' for growth, employment, equity and efficiency: Phase II. Retrieved October 23, 2020, from www.ilo.org/wcmsp5/groups/public/-asia/-ro-bangkok/-sro-bangkok/documents/genericdocument/wcms_112939.pdf

Sen, H. (2013). *'Rectangular strategy' for growth, employment, equity and efficiency: Phase III* (pp. 1–42, Rep.). Phnom Penh, Cambodia: Royal Government of Cambodia.

Sen, H. (2018). *Rectangular strategy for growth, employment, equity and efficiency: Building the foundation toward realizing the Cambodia vision 2050: Phase IV* (pp. 1–46, Rep.). Phnom Penh, Cambodia: Royal Government of Cambodia.

Siddiquee, N. A. (2006). Public management reform in Malaysia: Recent initiatives and experiences. *International Journal of Public Sector Management, 19*(4), 339–358. doi:10.1108/09513550610669185

Siffin, W. (1976). Two decades of public administration in developing countries. *Public Administration Review, 36*(1), 61–71.

Silzer, R., & Church, A. H. (2009). The pearls and perils of identifying potential. *Industrial and Organizational Psychology, 2*(4), 377–412.

Singapore Tourism Board. (2021). Management associate programme. Retrieved January 15, 2021, from www.stb.gov.sg/content/stb/en/careers/students-and-fresh-graduates/management-associate-programme.html

Sivanandam, H. (2012). Malaysia remuneration system reinstated, new pay scheme abolished. *The Sun Daily.* Retrieved January 3, 2021, from http://

cuepacs.blogspot.com/2012/03/malaysia-remuneration-system-reinstated. html

Sivaraks, P. (2011). Civil service system in Thailand. In E. Berman (Ed.), *Public administration in Southeast Asia: Thailand, Philippines, Malaysia, Hong Kong and Macao* (pp. 113–140). Boca Raton, FL: CRC Press.

Socheath, S. (2020). Gov't to recruit over 6,000 civil servants next year. *Khmer Times*. Retrieved from www.khmertimeskh.com/50783383/govt-to-recruit-over-6000-civil-servants-next-year/

Sok, S. (2013). *Better governance: Human resource policy within Cambodia's public administration* (pp. 1–5, Rep.). Seoul, Korea: OECD Korea Policy Centre.

Sophanith, P. (2020). France reiterates support for Cambodia's civil servant capacity building. *Khmer Times*. Retrieved from www.khmertimeskh.com/50764796/france-reiterates-support-for-cambodias-civil-servant-capacity-building/

Stahl, B., Fardale, I., & Morris, E. (2012). Six principles of effective global talent management. *MIT Sloan Management Review, 53,* 24–32.

Sumonta, P., Finley, F., & Kaweekijmanee, K. (2018). The evolution and current status of STEM education in Thailand: Policy directions and recommendations. In W. F. Gerald (Ed.), *Education in Thailand: An old elephant in search of a new mahout* (pp. 423–460). Minneapolis, MN: Springer.

Sun, X., & Ross, C. (2009). The training of Chinese managers: A critical analysis of using overseas training for management development. *Journal of Chinese Economic and Business Studies, 7*(1), 95–113.

Swailes, S. (2013). Troubling some assumptions: A response to 'The role of perceived organizational justice in shaping the outcomes of talent management: A research agenda'. *Human Resource Management Review, 23*(4), 354–356.

Swailes, S., & Blackburn, M. (2016). Employee Reactions to Talent Pool Membership. *Employee Relations, 38*(1), 112–128.

Swailes, S., Downs, Y., & Orr, K. (2014). Conceptualising inclusive talent management: Potential, possibilities and practicalities. *Human Resource Development International, 17*(5), 529–544.

Tamronglak, A. (2020). Impacts of the Thailand qualification framework: Public administration on public administration education in Thailand. *Journal of Public Affairs Education, 26*(3), 276–290.

Tan, K. P. (2008). Meritocracy and elitism in a global city: Ideological shifts in Singapore. *International Political Science Review, 29,* 7–27.

Tan, K. S., & Bhaskaran, M. (2015). The role of the state in Singapore: Pragmatism in pursuit of growth. *Singapore Economic Review, 60*(3), 1–30.

Tansley, C. (2011). What do we mean by 'talent' in talent management? *Industrial and Commercial Training, 43*(5), 266–274.

Tansley, C., Turner, P., & Foster, C. (2007). *Talent Strategy, Management, Measurement.* London: CIPD.

Tansley, C., Harris, L., Stewart, K., Turner, P., Foster, C., & Williams, H. (2006). *Talent management: Understanding the dimensions.* London: CIPD.

Taylor, W. A., & Wright, G. (2004). Organizational readiness for successful knowledge sharing: Challenges for public sector managers. *Information Resources Management Journal*, *17*(2), 22–37.

Thailand Development Research Institute (TDRI). (2014). Economic impact from the 300 baht minimum wage policy and 15,000 baht salary for Bachelor's degree graduates.

Thunnissen, M., Boselie, P., & Fruytier, B. (2013). A review of talent management: 'Infancy or adolescence?'. *The International Journal of Human Resource Management*, *24*(9), 1744–1761.

Thunnissen, M., & Buttiens, D. (2017). Talent management in public sector organizations: A study on the impact of contextual factors on the TM approach in Flemish and Dutch public sector organizations. *Public Personnel Management*, *46*(4), 391–418.

Tilman, R. O. (1961). Public service commissions in the Federation of Malaya. *The Journal of Asian Studies*, *20*(2), 181–196. doi:10.2307/2050482

Ulrich, D. (2006). The talent trifecta. *Workforce Management*, 32–33.

Ulrich D., & Smallwood, N. (2012). What is Talent? *Leader to Leader*, *63*, 55–61.

Ulrich, D., & Ulrich, M. (2010). *Marshalling talent*. Paper at the 2010 Academy of Management Annual Meeting, Montreal.

United Nations Development Programme. (2016). *Scaling-up south-south cooperation for sustainable development* (Rep.). New York, NY: United Nations Development Programme.

Universum. (2020). The world's most attractive employer 2020. Retrieved December 15, 2020, from https://universumglobal.com/blog/the-worlds-most-attarctive-employer 2020/#:~:text=In%202020%2C%20among%20 the%20companies,Mosley%2C%20chief%20strategist%20at%20Universum

Vaiman, V., & Collings, D. (2013). Talent management: Issues of focus and fit. *The International Journal of Human Resource Management*, *24*(9), 1737–1743.

Vakkuri, J., & Meklin, P. (2006). Ambiguity in performance measurement: A theoretical approach to organisational uses of performance measurement. *Financial Accountability and Management*, *22*(3), 235–250.

Vandeluxe, Y. (2014). Chapter 3: Historical development of administrative law in Cambodia. In K. Hauerstein & J. Menzel (Eds.), *The development of Cambodian administrative law* (pp. 105–114). Phnom Penh, Cambodia: Konrad-Adenauer-Stiftung.

Van den Brink, M., Fruytier, B., & Thunnissen, M. (2013). Talent management in academia: Performance systems and HRM policies. *Human Resource Management Journal*, *23*(2), 180–195.

Van Dijk, H. (2009). Administration vs. talent: The administrative context for talent management. *Journal of Public Administration*, *44*(3), 520–530.

Vietnam Ministry of Home Affairs. (2018). *Thông tư số 01/2018/TT-BNV ngày 08/01/2018 của Bộ Nội vụ về hướng dẫn thực hiện một số điều của Nghị định số 101/2017/NĐ-CP ngày 01/9/2017 của Chính phủ về đào tạo, bồi dưỡng cán bộ, công chức, viên chức (Circular No. 01/2018/TT-BNV dated 8/1/2018 on guidelines for the articles in Decree No. 101/2017/NĐ-CP by the government on the training and retraining of officials and civil servants).* Hanoi: Vietnam Ministry of Home Affairs.

Von Seldeneck, M. J. (2004). Finding an hiring fast-track talent. In L. A. Berger & D. R. Berger (Eds.), *The talent management handbook: Creating organisational excellence by identifying, developing and promoting your best people.* New York: McGraw-Hill.

Wah, Y. K. (1980). The grooming of an elite: Malay administrators in the federated Malay states, 1903–1941. *Journal of Southeast Asian Studies, 11*(2), 287–319. doi:10.1017/s0022463400004483

Woo, K. (2015). Recruitment practices in the Malaysian public sector: Innovations or political responses? *Journal of Public Affairs Education, 21*(2), 229–246.

World Bank. (2013). Public Service Pay in Cambodia: the Challenges of Salary Reform. Cambodia policy note; public sector reforms. Washington, D.C.: World Bank Group.

World Bank. (2017). *Vietnam Public Expenditure Review: Summary Report.* Washington, D.C.: World Bank Group.

World Bank. (2019). The World Bank in Singapore. Retrieved from www.worldbank.org/en/country/singapore/overview

World Bank. (2020, March 20). *Scaling up social accountability in key public services in Cambodia* (Press release). Phnom Penh: World Bank Group.

World Bank Group. (2018). *Cambodia's cross cutting reforms: Public financial management, decentralization, and public administration reforms: Achievements, coordination, challenges, and next steps* (Rep.). Phnom Penh, Cambodia: The World Bank.

Xinhua. (2020). 41 pct of civil servants in Cambodia female. *Xinhua Net.* Retrieved from www.xinhuanet.com/english/2020-02/17/c_138792749.htm

Yarnal, A., & Annapoorna, M. (2017). Review of literature on 'talent management'. *AARMSS International Journal of Management and Social Sciences Research, 3*(2), 23–41.

Yavaprabhas, S. (2018). Leadership and public sector reform in Thailand. In E. Berman & E. Prasojo (Eds.), *Leadership and public sector reform in Asia* (Vol. 30, Public policy and governance, pp. 103–126). Bingley, UK: Emerald Publishing Limited.

Yost, P. R., & Chang, G. (2009). Everyone is equal, but some are more equal than others. *Industrial and Organizational Psychology: Perspectives on Science and Practice, 2*, 442–445.

Young, M. (1958). *The rise of the meritocracy 1870–2033: An essay on education and society.* London: Thames and Hudson.

Zhao, L., & Wong, J. (2013). Singapore's social development experience: A relevant lesson for China? In L. Zhao (Ed.), *China's Social Development and Policy: Into the Next Stage.* London: Routledge.

Index

Note: Page numbers in *italics* indicate a figure and page numbers in **bold** indicate a table on the corresponding page.